W9-DIS-300

The Expanded Mission of City Center Churches

Ray Bakke
Sam Roberts

To purchase additional copies of
THE EXPANDED MISSION OF CITY CENTER CHURCHES,
Call, write or fax your order to:

International Urban Associates
5151 N. Clark Street, 2nd Floor
Chicago, IL 60640-2829

Phone: (773) 275-9260
Fax: (773) 275-9969

Published by International Urban Associates
5151 N. Clark Street, 2nd Floor
Chicago, IL 60640-2829

Printed in the United States of America

Library of Congress Cataloging-in-Publication Data
Bakke, Raymond J., 1938-
    The Expanded Mission of City Center Churches

    Bibliography: p.
    1. City Churches—United States. 2. Church renewal—
Baptists. 3. Baptists—United States—History.
I. Roberts, Samuel K. II. Title.
ISBN 0-9664671-0-8

Contents

Preface

For several years now, our many colleagues and ministry students in various pastoral settings have told us that this book should be both republished and renamed. The earlier title, "The Expanded Mission of 'Old First' Churches" contained the thesis of the book, but it was neutral in terms of the city-center context. We were and are yet convinced that traditional city center churches often labor under the assumption that city centers were places to be abandoned. It is true that for a generation cities have ripped out or paved over huge sections of their downtown cores, but for a variety of reasons, that is not the trend of the future. Everyone now realizes that abandoning city center was a great mistake—producing a city, which like a donut, had vital edges but a hole in the center. "Old First" churches looked like beached whales when the tide went out. Many in fact did sell their buildings and relocate.

City centers always had political, economic and cultural roles, but those were altered by shifts from heavy to light industry and now the growth of financial and high tech businesses which are reshaping the metroplex. Joel Garreau is not alone in believing that the new downtown is where the Interstate highways intersect.[1]

Increasingly, however, cities are committed to the repopulating of city centers. Paris and New York City are but two examples of cities that did not abandon their core centers, and they are the new models for cities all over the world. Denver is but one of many examples of cities that have recommitted themselves to bringing the children of the suburbs back downtown. But there is more. We live at a time in human history during which some of the greatest people migrations are taking place. As a result, cities around the world are becoming the catch basins of the nations.

So, in this book we are reaffirming a basic fact that emerged from our data. Turning around old churches is not fundamentally different in suburban, small town or rural communities. The principles identified in our research work across those boundaries and do not change significantly from large city to county seat town. The difference is one of degree. Urbanization is the concentration of cities in places, but urbanism is the spread of urban lifestyles in the media-driven culture of the West, and that continues everywhere. There is hardly any geographical real estate now that can escape the spread of our cities. Cities point the way to the future. They are like the time-lapse camera. They speed up reality. We study cities, not because they are so different from rural areas, but for the opposite reason: they help us prepare for tomorrow in non-city communities.

In the reality we are describing then, city churches are like "R & D" units (research and development), for the rest of society and for all denominations. City centers are changing, but social pluralism is still a fundamental characteristic of their environment. Along with that is the equally significant fact that nearly all of life at city center is institutionalized or packaged by forces in and outside the area. City centers are not human-scale communities. They are larger than life. They are multi-generational institutions, pyramids of power and decision-making on a grand, new international scale. The church at city center operates with these contextual realities as a given. And while the functions of every church in the world are always the same—worship, evangelism, discipleship, stewardship, fellowship and service—the forms those functions take will necessarily adapt to their unique context. So, pastoring the city center church remains an art (not a science) practiced at profound levels.

Why We Republish This Book

In the years since we published "The Expanded Mission of 'Old First' Churches," we have witnessed a veritable explosion of books on churches and pastors. Like our peers, we have read them and profited greatly. Organizational behavior and management science have had a profound effect on pastors and denominations in the past two decades. But, it has also become increasingly clear to us why this little book was so powerfully compelling to those who read it in the mid-1980s, and why it is still unique today.

First, this is above all a theology book about the nature and mission of the church viewed both historically and currently. It integrates theological reflection and sociological data in a way that church leaders can access and use to understand their own congregational practices. It is more than a "how-to manual." Moreover, it really is not just a pastor's book. It was designed to be read by the leadership team of the church over a period of time. Most church studies have a pragmatic feel about them. If it works and churches grow, then we should follow the guidelines. This is not that kind of book. This book assumes the church is God's and not ours, and that the church's principles may be dissonant with the dominant culture or trends at given times.

A second uniqueness of this book is that it assumes a multi-generational perspective. Tall steeple churches were not single generation institutions. They were Protestant equivalents of cathedrals. They were placed downtown originally as "chaplains to power." They ministered to "boulevard people" rather than "side-street people." The theological concept that tall steeples elicit in us is transcendence. These members celebrated the "Christ over us" of Colossians, as well as the "Christ in us" of Philippians. They knew that the Christian faith is profoundly historical, meaning that God's glory will be seen over many generations, even when not necessarily in the membership statistics of any given year. The kingdom of God proclaims the good news that Christ's rule or lordship includes everything, not just the churches' sanctuaries or programs. Ministry in America has become increasingly autobiographical in that pastors are being taught to design ministry in their own images and around their own gifts, and often to focus their ministry on their own kind of people. That's not the case at city center. Like city mayors, pastors come and go over time. These churches are hard to change. That's the point. City center is a tough place. City center churches recycle around a common core of biblical values and congregational traditions that shaped identity over generations. While it is true that other churches need to speak powerfully to our ever-changing plastic and sound-bite culture, that is not the primary mission of city center churches. The leadership tool kit is different there. This book makes that point in a unique way.

A third uniqueness of this book centers around the fact that a decade ago "contextualization" was a word known only to mission theorists. Missionaries have always had the task of crossing difficult boundaries with the gospel. In the past that meant crossing oceans, jungles or mountains to plant sustainable churches in local cultures. Missionaries studied to understand cultures and languages, to take every context seriously. The incarnation of Christ into Galilean culture modeled it, and the Great Commission of the risen Christ mandated it. What we were saying in this book is that everything missionary scholars learned to do abroad, city center pastors must now do at home. We need to contextualize our ministry in the unique cultures of huge city center communities. We are not surprised to learn that missionaries in the past invented hospitals, schools, communications, and transportation systems and engaged in political dialogue as well as tribal conflict. Missionaries always operated beyond their gifts and outside their comfort zones. What we are saying is that nothing less is now demanded of churches at city center. The integrative pastoral discipline is missiology, for we have many things to learn about the "soils" into which we are attempting to plant our churches.

In the meantime, what we have come to know as "Liberation Theology," which has come out of Latin America primarily, has spread along with Pentecostalism all over the world. The fundamental truth of liberation theology is that God has agendas outside of the church, in the world, and truly desires the liberation of all peoples from every evil oppression. As such, liberation thinking should not frighten us at all. It has served as a corrective to the tendency of some Christians to be totally preoccupied with church structures, denominations and all things ecclesiastical. City center pastors know that the God who called the Persian King Cyrus "anointed" (Isa. 45:1ff), or enabled Nehemiah to access the government grant and gave him permission to do urban community organizing for the rebuilding of Jerusalem, will likewise involve them personally and professionally on the team for rebuilding the city center. City center pastors must blend personal faith and public faith, which assumes Christ's authority over all systems and structures of the city. Systems like health care, education, safety and a sound economy are what we might call gifts of "common grace," rather than "saving grace." They are paid out of taxes rather than our tithes, but all the money is in fact God's. Healthy persons need healthy families, and those families need healthy communities. The leaders of city center churches understand this. They can never limit their concerns to the evangelistic enterprise alone. They also must address the justice concerns of Scripture. They must be prophetic as well as pastoral to all the issues and institutions of city centers. While we affirm this, we have noticed that most church books published in recent years had little to say about their geographic environments; except perhaps, on how to exploit the environment for the church's benefit.

A fourth uniqueness of this book concerns the methodology used and the data discovered. We studied actual historic congregations in vastly diverse settings. This is not the report of one pastor or one church. We cite chapter and verse, as it were, in some 150 case studies, and we noticed common themes which wove their way through these stories about congregations as old as 300 years in some cases. We discovered and reported that there is hope for old churches. We said that if eight things occur, you can turn around an old first church.

By contrast, surely you have read books about superb churches, written by incredibly gifted and articulate pastors and found yourself saying things like: "But my situation is so different. I am so different also. I could never get away with doing that!" We can all profit by such books, of course. Success stories of megachurches are wonderful, especially those that walk us through the shadows and pain along the way to growth, so we can deal with reality en route to greatness.

Yet, unless readers clearly distinguish the principles that undergird such ministries, the tendency is to try and copy the patterns and programs of those congregations, regardless of one's own sociological context, theological tradition or ministry gifts. By contrast, the principles that emerged in this study clearly transcend contexts. The theory for turning around churches, while not claiming to be complete in this little book, offers some fresh thinking about God's church, and it comes from a wide variety of sources. No one therefore needs to say, "But we are not like them!"

Finally, we live at a time when race issues have surfaced again in a major way, impacting our whole country and each generation. The racial divides and misunderstandings, which were primarily visible in the South a generation ago, have emerged with a vengeance affecting many. For what it's worth, two men, Sam and Ray, one black and one white, did the research and then wrote this book. Not only did we design the initial survey to include black and white congregations, we wrote the book intentionally so that both African-American and Anglo-American congregations could read and use the material. We wrote from our respective Richmond and Chicago contexts, one as a sociologically trained ethicist and one as a historically oriented urbanologist. We were both pastors and seminary professors. Readers will find our disciplines integrated into each chapter, and we think you'd be surprised to know who wrote what, so closely was the agreement we shared in the final text.

We have decided not to change that original text. Except for a few updates in facts and language, this new "Preface" and an expansion of the "Epilogue" is all that has been altered in this new edition. So, once again, we share the fruit of our labor—"what our hands have found to do, and what our hearts urge us yet to consider." We stand in awe of city center churches and their pastors, whom we consider our peers and colleagues in God's mission. We admire you so much. We hope also to encourage you.

Ray Bakke in Chicago and Sam Roberts in Richmond
Pentecost 1998

The Problem and Promise
of Old First Church

Old First is rooted in a time in American history when the heartland of this country was opening to the frontierspeople, and small communities of believers moved to meet God in the wilderness. Most of the churches in this study were begun by believers who were caught up in the evangelical fervor of the Second Great Awakening, or the period in American church history roughly from 1820 to 1850. This company of believers was characterized as having strong, forceful, and enlightened leaders as pastors, and equally committed laypersons. After a period of worshiping in a home, they constructed an edifice that was usually rather imposing in the context of the times and place. Even a wooden structure adorned by a simple but sturdy steeple had an air of grandeur on the frontier. The red brick edifice, put squarely in the hub of a frontier town, was a sign of stability, a sign of God in the midst of a people struggling to bring order out of the wilderness. There was a sense among these Old First churches that the destiny of the church was closely linked with the peculiar set of circumstances inherent in God's providential order.

These Old First churches were highly sensitive to the social issues prevalent at the time, issues they believed God was leading them to confront. Slavery and temperance were extremely volatile issues to which the highly disciplined band of believers in these churches directed their energy and resolve. Such commitment and zeal for social change had a foundation in the theological orientation of the founders of Old Firsts. They believed that God was at work in history and that justice and right could not prevail except through the efforts of the people of faith. They furthermore believed that human beings, as creatures of God, could be converted to the cause of God, goodness, salvation, and social uplift. It was therefore consistent with their faith understanding that the founders of Old First churches—both pastors and members—could be champions of the development of the intellect, active in what they perceived to be just moral causes, and steadfast in the arena of public uplift. Such values were not only transmitted to other persons and institutions in the community in which these Old First churches were planted, but also to succeeding generations. One therefore finds within Old First churches—at least until the mid-twentieth century—a distinct pattern of two and three generations of the same family within the same church. Old First churches were visible symbols of stability when all else was turbulent.

Old First churches were closely linked, perhaps too closely, to the powerful and wealthy in American communities. They endeavored—and sometimes failed—to serve as the conscience of the rising middle classes and the persons of means who formed the social elite in communities. In return for providing a spiritual home for such persons, Old Firsts were rewarded in bequests and wills to such an extent that endowments, trusts, and other legacies became a noted feature in the fiscal structure of many of these churches throughout the nineteenth century. These financial foundations account for the very existence of some churches to this day.

Old Firsts have now come upon hard times. Their once thriving memberships became depleted when countless members chased the "American Dream" to the outer fringes of the suburbs. The large, magnificent edifices, so imposing in their grandeur in an earlier time, now appear forlorn as row upon row of empty pews give mute testimony to a faded glory. The few worshipers who do return on Sunday out of a sense of loyalty must now pass sullen neighbors who, despite living in close proximity to the church, do not feel that it is "their" church. Old Firsts seem forgotten by the wealthy and expendable to the men and women in power—so unlike an earlier time when the powerful needed membership in Old Firsts as a part of their respectability.

The Old First church is an exceedingly complex phenomenon. Positive images that such a church might evoke are its historic grandeur, its visionary and courageous pastoral leadership offering dynamic preaching to the rich and powerful, its stability in communities, and its flagship congregations—the veritable jewels in the denominational crown. On the other hand, there were the negative images: very formal worship services attended by very formal people who listened to very formal church music, and an ethos that was bound to tradition and did not make room for people of another background.

Old First is full of history that bespeaks the presence of saints, sinners, the pompous, and the penitent. It is much like the church universal or redeemed humanity in general, but a very special segment of the church with great potential!

The authors share a common thesis that there is a future and a hope for Old Firsts to recover the freshness of the vision of their founders. To do so, however, Old Firsts will have to embody a theological perspective of being the incarnational presence of Christ in a community, planted there to help redeem people and place. We believe the future is bright for the Old First churches that can come to terms with their social context and not attempt to escape it. Sensitivity to context will mean that Old Firsts will not be afraid to modify their internal structures or to redefine the parameters of the meaning of membership within the body. The future is bright for the Old Firsts that can recover the public mission of the church, not so much by being chaplains of the powerful but by securing the trust of the public. Bold pastoral and lay leadership and the courage to speak knowingly and passionately on the great issues that concern people will go a long way toward gaining their trust. As the chapters of this book will suggest in greater detail, we believe that there is a viable future for Old Firsts if the following conditions prevail:

1. If there is quality *lay and professional leadership* within the ranks of Old First churches.

2. If a sound *theological perspective* is developed on biblical mission, values, goals, context, and community of the Old First and put into place.

3. If a functional *history* of Old Firsts can be recovered; if Old Firsts can redeem their usable pasts.

4. If a *mission* which is genuinely contextualized can be developed that shows that Old Firsts can adjust to new dynamics and new opportunities.

5. If bulky and worn-out *structures* can be streamlined and refocused.

6. If *programs* can be ranked to reflect the conscious mobilization and empowerment of church members and the stewardship of their unique gifts for ministry.

This book is written primarily for the church. It is written for all who struggle to bear witness to the continuing life of Christ in the church, wherever that church may be found. Yet in a very real sense we have discovered that in the course of research for this book, and in conversations with key persons in these Old Firsts, issues that go to the very heart of American culture have been raised. Such a discovery also helps answer the question "Why this book at this time?"

We believe that there are three fundamental reasons why this book is crucial at this juncture in the history of American churches and American culture. The first reason speaks to an issue that is really at the heart of the contemporary American mind-set. Americans are uncomfortable with persons and institutions that are aged and aging. Our current fashion of referring to some of us as "senior citizens" instead of simply "old people" or "elders" belies an attempt to sanitize an unspeakable embarrassment: that among us are some people whose forms are more feeble than others and whose bodies are less supple. Such people do not look good on magazine covers nor do they keep up very well with people on the go. The sight of an Old First church, now covered with grime and ash on an abandoned block of an inner city, may constitute a similar embarrassment for church members and denominational leaders. This book is a plea for a reevaluation of origins and a recovery of roots. It is a cry against the prevalent narcissism in our culture wherein upwardly mobile individuals sever ties with roots and the generation that spawned them and with the ground that gave them a sense of place in the scheme of things. In this book Old Firsts will be encouraged to shed any embarrassment about their age and celebrate the fact that they, like the elders in our society, have endured.

The second reason for this book has to do with a prevalent "single-issue" syndrome within some quarters of American churches and society. There is a dangerous superficiality at work in this land which reduces failure and success to a single issue or reason. Special interest groups feed on this syndrome, and myopic leaders exploit it. As the array of issues treated under various chapter headings in this book will suggest, the treatment of Old Firsts cannot be reduced to one simple issue. The issues are as complex and interrelated as the world in which we live.

Finally, this book is written at this particular time because of the relationship between the rate of social change in the world today and the concept of missions. Missions in the church have normally been associated with the practice of churches in the West taking the gospel to people in exotic parts of the world. However, due to vast social upheavals and economic dislocations that have occurred in our world, the former recipients of the gospel from east and south of the equator have moved west and north. The presence of Haitians in Brooklyn and Arabs in Chicago gives ample testimony to the changed context of foreign missions. We believe that the recovery of mission for Old Firsts may in fact be the harbinger of the way the twenty-first century church will have to rearrange its priorities and deploy its resources in order to minister to a truly global society right next door!

While much of American society encourages narcissistic pursuit of pleasure and profit, historic Old First churches herald a community and corporate life ethic. While scientific technology and human wastefulness have encouraged the development of a plastic, throwaway culture that mars our environment, Old Firsts maintain a commitment to place and natural materials. Old Firsts know the folly of popular single-generation fads; multigenerational values and identity strengthen Old Firsts.

Readers may object to possible caricatures in the differentiation between American society and the Old First ethic. Generalizations are generally wrong, but reflections on these Old First values (which we admit were not universally assumed in all Old Firsts) tell us something about the Christian faith and mission of those who built these Old First churches that is largely missing today.

"Heresies," as William Temple has often said, "are exaggerations of truth," which, we might add, lead to the consequent neglect of other truths. We surely do not hunger for museum churches as such, nor is nostalgia the motivation for our hope that Old Firsts will recover their vision and mission for today. Rather, it is our belief that revitalization may prove to be the most radical solution for contemporary ills. A renewed Old First is needed today. There must be some place in the community of constant change where the church can be a sign and agent of God's kingdom and can witness to those things that do not change. There must be a place where theology and mission can exist to give shape, identity, and hope to people across race and language groups. The authors believe that in the flower garden of God's kingdom, Old Firsts can recover and bloom again with valuable consequences for the other churches around them.

Chapter 1

Using History to Recover Vision

The rise and fall of Old First churches is a drama of epic proportions. The churches in this study take on heroic postures when one considers the trials they overcame to assert their faith in the context of persecution and to maintain their precarious existence on the frontier and at the edge of the wilderness. Amid these tribulations the men and women who founded these churches manifested a keenness of faith and trust in God that now must shame persons of lesser fortitude. The questions now come to those persons who hope to do ministry in and for Old Firsts today: How do we recover the radical vision of the founders? How can we recover the freshness of the call to mission that fired the hearts and souls of the earliest members of Old First churches? This book is an attempt to help persons in such situations discover some answers to these crucial questions.

In attempting to recover the vision of the founders of an Old First church, it is important to begin by understanding and appreciating that church's past. History is a unique fabric of human vision brought to fruition within the context of human effort. Different factors accounted for the reason some Old Firsts were planted on the prairie or in the wilderness, some in a colonial city, and others on a river near a growing town. History is the confluence of many elements: favorable circumstances, environment, uniqueness of people, and the fidelity of one generation to the mandates of the prior generation. History tends to guard very closely its secrets.

Moreover, there is no sure way of determining what was going on in the minds of the original actors, in this case the people who founded these churches. We must approach history with awe and respect, for we stand before events that we do not fully understand. We can only give celebratory thanks for them.

The prophets in the Old Testament consistently said to Israel, "Remember when we were in Egypt, remember when God delivered us." They understood the power of remembering as the primary antidote to survivor mentalities. The powerful fact to remember is that without a functioning memory, no institution or individual can truly prepare for the future. In a sense then, one *remembers* the future.

This chapter introduces the heritage of Baptist Old First congregations, not researched from primary source documents in libraries, but recovered from contemporary members of those congregations as they presented their own case studies.

The authors of this book share a fundamental operating assumption that has gained acceptance across denominational lines in recent decades. Sensitivity to the power of history shows the relativity and temporality of the historic structures that have been handed down to us. Historical consciousness raises basic hermeneutical questions that allow us to question and reinterpret Old Firsts and all other churches in radical ways. How are we to interpret present and past events which will have import for the future?

What follows is a narrative of historical vignettes as remembered by congregations that are learning to tell their own stories. Read this chapter, not for the complete record of church historical data, but to see how Old Firsts have begun to dig their own roots and sort out the transferable concepts or principles that give them identity and energy today. We are not saying that history is a "wax nose" to be molded into whatever shape we want. Nor are we saying that churches should invent a past. We are suggesting that congregations study their own histories. In doing so, they should gather the old sources and develop a chronology of congregational life and mission up to the present. The real stuff of this study, however, is not just remembering that the church bought the property downtown in 1827 or that it built a huge sanctuary in 1874 and a Christian education unit in 1952, but recalling *why* the congregation did those things. What can you learn from the records about the vision of that congregation that led them to do what they did? Why did they network and develop associations? Why did they build buildings, budgets, and institutions the way they did? What were their hopes and dreams? What was the essence of their theology of mission?

When congregations reflect on their unique histories, they are freed up to find key themes or motifs that operated throughout their past. These motifs are their heritage. A principle of outreach may have led them to build a gym in 1910, but may not lead to that decision today. However, the same principle of outreach may lead the church to become multilingual in the present day. The heritage of Old Firsts is much more than old buildings and frozen systems. The key to renewal is opening up the story of the past. Our goal is not an exercise in nostalgia, but the recovery of faith and vision that is embedded in the current structures.

There will always be more work for the serious historians in the rich traditions of Old Firsts, many of whom have historical collections, doubtless in disarray. Nevertheless, as you read the following narratives reconstructed here from some fifty historical cases, try to identify and classify the major themes that emerge from the stories. Your own congregation may illustrate these same motifs, adding others and recognizing that some do not pertain to your situation.

Stories from the Archives of Old Firsts

A vital part of the heritage of the American churches lies in a world outside the United States: the religious wars of Europe, the bitter experiences of exploitation and colonization in Africa and Asia, and the ferment of socioeconomic transformations of Latin America. At the same time, another part of that heritage stems from the experience in the United States: the confrontation with the wilderness and frontier; the conflict of cultures and colors—white, black, yellow, brown, and red—and the hope for building the kingdom of God in the New World. The peculiar history of American Baptist churches and particularly these Old First churches resonates to the vibrations of these two poles in the heritage of the American churches.

Baptists can be traced to the historic stand of believers who sought to separate themselves from the established faiths of Europe during the seventeenth century. Hence, the history of the Baptists is inextricably linked to those "Separatists" who risked life, fortune, and status in their escape from the tyranny of state supported churches. Such tyranny had dogged the existence of Separatists in their struggle against Anglicans in England and the Catholics in Spain and France.

After seeking refuge from religious persecution in Holland and England, the Puritan Separatists who settled in the Massachusetts Bay Colony proceeded to establish their own religious dogma as the only legitimate faith of the land. The Separatists were as relentless as their former persecutors had been. They, too, ridiculed, jailed, and persecuted others—particularly Baptists. Prominent among the latter during the early seventeenth century was Roger Williams. After a series of stormy encounters with the Puritans of Boston between 1631 and 1634, a Boston court finally declared: "Whereas Mr. Roger Williams...hath broached and divulged diverse new and dangerous opinions against the authority of the magistrates and churches here...it is therefore ordered that the said Mr. Williams shall depart out of this jurisdiction...."[1] Williams left the Bay Colony for the headwaters of the Narragansett Bay and founded a settlement there, naming it "Providence," "in a sense of God's merciful providence to me in my distress."[2] After Williams purchased land from the nearby

Indians as a haven for people seeking religious freedom, other Separatists, dissenters, and Baptists began to drift into the settlement. In 1638 Williams and these seekers of religious freedom founded the first Baptist church in America.

Quite literally then, the "first" Baptist church in America was planted in the soil of the quest for religious freedom. Still defiant of the religious authorities of the Massachusetts Bay Colony, seven men and two women came together on June 7, 1665, to form the First Baptist Church of Boston, Massachusetts.[3] They were banished from the colony because of their religious faith. The first pastor, Mr. Thomas Gould, was considered an outlaw until the time of his death. Five of the seven men who were charter members were imprisoned at one time or another. By the time of the Revolution, however, the organization was established, and there were about sixty members on the roll. Such quests for religious freedom were not confined to the Massachusetts Bay Colony. Other colonies and cities along the Atlantic Coast were also infused with the intense fervor for religious freedom which resulted in the formation of Baptist churches.

Also growing out of this religious fervor, the First Baptist Church of Philadelphia[4] was formed on the second Sunday in December 1698, when nine Baptists gathered in a storehouse near the banks of the Delaware River. William Penn had founded the city only sixteen years before. Since 1695 this small band had been meeting jointly with some Presbyterians who apparently were of Separatist mind. In a real sense, however, the "mother church" of First Baptist Church of Philadelphia can be traced to a gathering of Baptists in 1688, led by the Reverend Elias Keech, minister of the nearby church in Pennepack. First Baptist of Philadelphia would spawn many other movements and institutions, among them the first association of Baptist churches in America, the Philadelphia Baptist Association, organized in 1707. This "associational impulse" among Baptists was no doubt the result of a need to bear witness to a faith which could not be suppressed by established structures but which nevertheless needed the supportive networks that groups of like-minded believers could provide.

The network and the ferment of witnessing before and on behalf of believers took on astounding energy and scope after the first quarter of the eighteenth century. This period has been rightly called the "First Great Awakening" in American church history. Perhaps no other religious phenomenon during this century had the scope and intensity to produce such far-reaching transformations as did the First Great Awakening. The Awakening began in 1726 in the Raritan Valley of New Jersey among Dutch Reformed circles under the leadership of Theodore J. Frelinghuysen. Under Frelinghuysen's leadership, the movement transformed the Dutch Reformed churches, many of which had grown rather staid, representing merely the symbols of the cultural heritage and history of the ethnic Dutch. Among the Presbyterians, the Awakening divided those who held that current belief and adherence to the Westminster Confession (Old Lights) was enough for salvation from those who believed in the power of experiential religion (New Lights). It was perhaps among the Baptists that the Awakening would have its most profound effect and for whom the dividends, in terms of converts, would be most obvious. This was because the thrust of the Awakening—the emphasis on experiential faith and corresponding emotional fervor—resonated deeply in the hearts of Baptists. This resonance would manifest itself throughout the years of the First Great Awakening and indeed throughout the remaining years of the eighteenth century.

Although most of the churches in this study were founded during the Second Great Awakening, the First Great Awakening also caused many Baptist churches to be planted. Pushing its way beyond the confines of New England and into the Middle Atlantic states and the wilderness of western New York, the Awakening led to the founding of eighteen Baptist churches in New Jersey by 1785. One of these churches eventually became the Hamilton Square Baptist Church,[5] which owes its beginning to the early ministry and witness of Morgan Edwards. The former pastor at First Baptist Church of Philadelphia, Edwards was "a man to be wondered at." Edwards began to preach in Nottingham Square, New Jersey, in 1785. A little gathering of believers began to meet in homes. Soon thereafter they erected a meetinghouse. On April 25, 1789, "They agreed to hold communion at Nottingham the second Lord's Day in March, June, September, and December." Believers were baptized during the earliest years of the church in James Hutchinson's mill pond. Other churches in New Jersey began to be planted by Baptists toward the latter years of the eighteenth century. The First Baptist Church of Flemington was formed when fifteen people covenanted together on June 19, 1798.[6]

The growth in the number of First churches among Baptists during these years was due to the march of settlers into the wilderness, primarily the western parts of New York State. For example, the first settlers of Hamilton, New York (earlier called Payne's Settlement, after the man who led the settlers), were Baptists. Two years later (in 1796) the church was organized, and six years later the members called a pastor who was a veteran of the Revolutionary War.[7] Similarly, Baptist settlers in Ossining, New York, came to that part of the state in 1786. They began meeting in the home of Captain Elijah Hunter before incorporating themselves as a church in 1790. They covenanted together in a time "when there was a newness and freshness to the spirit of the people."[8] The associational impulse among Baptists on the frontier accounted for the genesis of the First Baptist Church of Oneonta, New York.[9] This church came into being in 1833 from an association of Baptists called the Franklin Baptist Association, formed in 1795. The birth of the First Baptist Church of Watertown, New York, in 1823 was also the product of an associational impulse, in this case the Black River Association, at which the delegates signed a covenant together.[10]

Baptists also came together out of an intense sense of revivalism, both in the established settlements of the time and also in an effort to evangelize the unchurched in the wilderness settings. On June 18, 1796, several intrepid souls covenanted with one another to work together as a gospel church. In 1807 the leaders of the First Baptist Church of Hamilton, New York, founded the Lake Baptist Missionary Society to evangelize the frontier as it spread westward through the state.[11] Later this same church would be instrumental in taking a leadership role in founding a mission to the Oneida Indians, underwriting the cost of a missionary teacher/preacher and the cost of constructing a church, school, parsonage, blacksmith's shop, and carpentry shop on the reservation. An unabashed wish that there be a "Baptist witness in the county seat" led eleven people to form the First Baptist Church of Mount Vernon, New York.[12] A few believers began meeting among themselves in 1821 for prayer and a year later began to institute Sunday meetings. Later in that same year they organized the church, declaring that a Baptist church would be "profitable to Zion."

In the late 1820s a new wave of revivalism swept across the country with all the intensity of the First Great Awakening. There were significant differences, however. The Second Great Awakening placed an emphasis on humanitarian concerns, the use of freedom to improve the human situation, and a general optimism with regard to the world and human condition.[13] Of course, some Baptist churches took stands against slavery long before the Second Great Awakening. A good example of this is the story of the founding of the Bethel Baptist Church in Bethel, Ohio.

In 1796, Obed Denham, a native of Plainfield, New Jersey, who had lived for a few years in Kentucky and had become relentlessly opposed to human slavery, made deliberate plans to escape from all associations with the slave traffic. He set out to found a permanent home in the freedom of the unbroken forests in what is now the state of Ohio. Accompanied by his wife, six children, and other family members, he crossed the Ohio River in 1796 and purchased fifteen hundred acres of land in what is now Tate Township, Clermont County, Ohio. There he founded a congenial community for people who shared his opinion about slavery. Fellowship was refused to anyone who had any sympathy for slavery.[14] As early as 1806 this community appointed Obed's brother John as a messenger to the Emancipation Association, an antislavery organization in Ohio. In nearby West Virginia the founders of the First Baptist Church in Parkersburg boldly defied the racial customs of the day when seventeen white and seven black persons covenanted together to form a Baptist fellowship.[15]

While many Baptist churches willingly integrated white and black members in an organized show of religious solidarity, too many of them segregated their black congregants into an inferior status within the life of the church. Such a communion was the First Baptist Church of New York, then worshipping at Gold Street in New York City toward the beginning of the nineteenth century. The stirrings of protest against inferior status within this church later resulted in the formation of the Abyssinian Baptist Church of New York City.[16] Abyssinian was formed in 1808 after a radical white preacher named the Reverend Thomas Paul came from Boston to meet the small group of black worshipers who resented the segregation forced upon them by the white members of First Baptist Church. It is true also that while many white Baptists on the frontier, in the Ohio Valley, and in the Northwest Territories were adamantly opposed to slavery and saw the ethical mandate of accepting blacks as equals, local sentiment in many of these communities made it almost impossible for blacks to feel comfortable within some of the churches. This was the case in the First Baptist Church of Columbus, Ohio, formed in 1834. By that year the situation had become so unbearable for some blacks among the congregation that they petitioned to be "set aside" to form a church of their own. Consent was given and on January 6, 1834, the Second Baptist Church of Columbus came into existence.[17] In 1841 Second Baptist Church of Columbus led in the formation of the statewide Antislavery Association. The church itself became known among fugitive slaves as a way station on the Underground Railroad. In the Far West the often brittle ethnic conflicts that surfaced from time to time in the heady atmosphere of Gold Rush California caused blacks, many of whom were refugees from a life of persecution in the South and East, to form the Shiloh Baptist Church of Sacramento in 1856.[18]

As the American nation moved westward with each successive decade of the nineteenth century, so did the establishment of First churches among the Baptists. From the First Baptist Church of Boulder, Colorado,[19] organized to serve the miners of that settlement, to the First Baptist Church of Minneapolis, Minnesota,[20] founded in 1853 "in a prairie home," churches were established to meet specific needs occasioned by frontier life. The Kansas of the wild West saw the founding of the First Baptist Church of Wichita on May 26, 1872, when twenty-six persons gathered together, many representing the leadership spectrum of the community.[21] The founding of First Baptist Church of Minneapolis, Minnesota, was closely tied to the educational needs of the relatively unsettled prairie community. The service of this church would one day lead to the founding of Northwestern College in Roseville, Minnesota.

By the 1860s, the conquest of the wilderness (both in a spiritual and a commercial sense) and the winning of converts' hearts on the prairie would catapult Old First churches into a mode of ascendancy which would not diminish for nearly a century. Until the years after the Second World War these churches would wield much power, serving as "chaplains to the powerful." Old Firsts served as guardians of the values and morals of the leadership class of middle-class America, becoming symbols of all that was solid and dependable in American life.

Many of the internal wounds and fractures that had caused rifts in congregations during the formative years of the early nineteenth century were healed as the century reached its conclusion.

After reuniting two factions that had split in 1844, the forerunner of the First Baptist Church of Poughkeepsie, New York, formed an even stronger union in 1875 with a membership of 353.[22] This unified congregation was then fired with enthusiasm and steeled to the task of building an edifice that could seat six hundred people. In Hartford, Connecticut, the merger of South Baptist Church and the First Baptist Church of that city produced a formidable union in the emergent Central Baptist Church, formally organized in 1922. Earlier, however, in their own ways each church had begun to meet the unique challenges of doing ministry in its particular context. For example, First Baptist had begun an Italian and Russian mission in 1909. After the merger, the members moved to erect an edifice that would be "simple and functional in design" to symbolize their newfound strength. In 1925 a sanctuary seating 1,440 persons was built.[23] Throughout the first half of the twentieth century the church became a veritable beehive of activity, with various programs taking place within the 122 meeting, educational, and recreational rooms. Throughout this period the heartiness of outreach and mission was very much characteristic of Old First churches. Old First of Minneapolis, Minnesota, could seat three thousand people, and the members who attended on Sunday invariably filled the sanctuary. Similarly, Calvary Baptist Church of Washington, D.C., had reached a membership of 3,500 by the 1950s. Included in this membership were members of Congress, government workers, and many persons of means and influence.

The ascendancy of Old First churches during the first half of the twentieth century can be explained by the amount of service these churches provided for their communities. Thriving Sunday schools, midweek services, men's and women's Bible fellowships, literary societies, cultural arts guilds, and youth outreach programs were all extensions of Old Firsts into the community. Old Firsts could draw persons of power, means, and influence to their ranks. At the same time, Old Firsts provided the spiritual haven for persons who viewed themselves as leaders and pillars of the community. Old First churches, in their image and outreach, spoke to these peoples' self perceptions of power, influence, and respectability. Moreover, there was a sociological cohesion among the people of Old Firsts. They were primarily of middle- to upper-class income and family background. They were, for the most part, all white.

The vast social and economic changes which occurred in American society after World War II signaled the end of the First church as it was known in the first half of this century. Essentially, two social forces helped change the face of First church. First, the residential patterns of American life were radically changed with the trend toward suburbanization. While suburbs had been a noticeable feature of the urban landscape since the 1860s, only between 1920 and 1970 (and particularly after World War II) did their rate of growth begin to rival and finally exceed that of the inner cities they surrounded. The return of veterans was one of the factors that brought about a public housing policy opening up vast tracts of land surrounding the center city area for young families. Away from the congestion of the center city, the lure of a small patch of green backyard and the presence of essential support services such as schools and shopping markets were enough to persuade many young persons who could get a government-sponsored FHA (Federal Home Administration) loan to leave the city for the suburbs. The creation of the FHA in 1934 made home ownership in the suburbs accessible to more Americans than ever before. Furthermore, passage of the National Defense Highways Act in the 1950s ensured easy access to places of work in the cities. By 1970, a national census would show that more people were living in suburbs than were living in cities.

A second notable facet of the contemporary urban scene is the racial polarization that characterizes so many of our urban centers. While the suburban rings are still predominately white, inner cities are becoming increasingly populated by blacks and minority ethnic groups. At least two factors, one economic and the other sociological, contributed to these intense racial dynamics that are now so much a part of the urban scene. Part of the history of the economic factor began with the mechanization of farming as early as the 1870s. The refinement of farm machinery, such as the introduction of the harvester, meant that four men could do the work of fourteen. Increased mechanization in the twentieth century has meant that a smaller proportion of farm people, mainly in the South, can feed increasingly greater proportions of Americans, thus freeing a significant part of the population to seek out life in the cities. Mechanization meant that a sizable proportion of the traditional farm work force was made unnecessary and therefore economically marginal. In 1900, 90 percent of the black population resided in the South, and of this number close to 95 percent were rural. Southern blacks who migrated in increasing numbers to urban centers in the North and West during the years immediately after World War I were among these economically marginal people. The other factor which led to the racial dynamics of populations in the cities was the intense racial discrimination in the South and the brutal working conditions which white racism produced. Wave after wave of blacks migrated to the North in an attempt to escape the harsh reality of such oppression. In most cities the relations between the newcomers and the native whites were fraught with conflicts. The whites' reaction in most cases was that of either outright hostility or mild suspicion, followed by a move on their part to the suburbs. The end result of these migrations over a period of more than half a century and the resulting move of the whites to the suburbs surfaced in a disproportionate representation of blacks in the center areas of most of our cities.

It was in the context of these demographic and socioeconomic changes that Old First churches began a period of decline after World War II—a decline that would accelerate as the plight of the inner cities worsened. The particular plight of Old Firsts is reflected in diminished membership roles. While the main sanctuary of First Baptist Church in Philadelphia was designed to seat one thousand parishioners, the current membership is less than two hundred. Central Baptist Church of Boston still has an active membership close to five hundred, but this number must be put in the context of a sanctuary built to seat eleven hundred. Old First churches have met decline in lesser urban centers as well. First Baptist Church of Wichita, Kansas, is now in the midst of a dramatic revival in terms of membership after a period of decline two or three decades ago. First Baptist Church of Minneapolis, Minnesota, witnessed a radical change in neighborhoods surrounding the church and also a decline in membership in the 1960s.

Yet we can begin to understand the unique posture in which the founders of Old Firsts found themselves; we can "relive" history (as improbable as that seems) and we can do it in three ways. The first way is to appropriate fully the notion of "risk taking" in our approach to doing mission in the Old Firsts in which we have been placed. The original founders of Old Firsts were risk-takers. Risking the comfort of established and comfortable settings, the founders went into unknown and unsettled situations and areas. Our approach to the contemporary urban scene bespeaks a situation which is rather similar to the one faced by early settlers of areas from which Old Firsts grew. Many have spoken disparagingly of the "urban jungle." Enterprising young families who have sought to rehabilitate shabby housing in the inner city have come to see themselves as "urban homesteaders." While steel and concrete have replaced the sod of the western prairie, there is still the resolve to confront a new and awesome situation and make it better. The survivors who are still committed to Old Firsts have no less of a challenge than that of the original founders.

The second sense in which we may understand the original mission in the history of Old First is to understand the *intentionality* of the thrust into the wilderness. The founding of Old First in Minneapolis was not a lark or a casual expedition into an adventurous unknown; the founders perceived a real need for women and men of God to bring education to the prairie. The founding of this Old First was a *purposive* and *intentional* act, nurtured in a commitment to persons in real-life situations. This intentionality of purpose in early Old Firsts prevented a vague idealism or obscurity from settling over the posture of the church. It was clear what Old First stood for, whether it was the eradication of slavery or relief of loneliness of miners in early Colorado.

Finally, because Old Firsts have weathered many storms in their long sojourn through the past, they have been blessed with the gift of the long sweep of history. Old Firsts have seen the powerful come and go in their ranks; they have seen mill towns sprout, grow, and die. They have seen social fashions slip in and out of vogue. Graced with a posture that comes only with age, Old Firsts can now afford to take an unpopular stance on any issue for they know that popular conceptions of "rightness" are notoriously unreliable and illusory. Old Firsts can now care for those about whom no one else cares. They can speak to those to whom not a word has been uttered; they can be a presence for those devoid of human nurturing.

Thus the gift of history for Old First churches has within it at least three ways for these churches of old to recover their once thriving vitality: by taking risks, by intentionality of purpose, and by allowing freedom to do the unpopular. These things may not enable us to recreate the past, but if we fulfill them, what a past we would leave to others!

Other Histories Are Important, Too

Old Firsts are part of *national histories* as well. It is important to reflect on the local contextualized congregations and see the interplay of the larger environment. Migrations, wars, politics, and depressions were all part of the story as was the opening of regions by canals, railways, and roads. Our Baptist ancestors responded to these challenges in amazing ways.

Town or city histories are also important. The interplay of Old Firsts as "chaplains of power" in many instances can be seen by studying them in relationship to each other.

Personal histories are significant, too. Congregations would do well to collect oral histories of those who remember the past. Ask long-time members such questions as these:

- How did you come to your personal experience of Jesus Christ?
- How did you come to this church?
- What activities of this church do you remember with the greatest joy?
- If you could wave a wand and bring about a future for this church, what would it look like?

Then, let them talk. Tell those stories to the people in sermons and at celebrative times. It is amazing what stories of faith can do to bridge generations of members and what energies they can create. Even more amazing is the discovery that these sometimes stodgy, unchanging folks of today participated in radical activities in the past and did things they would criticize today.

You may discover that the same people who oppose a certain program or budget item today were the ones who promoted it back in 1947. Unlocking those memories can have interesting consequences. One reason older church members hold on to the morning service or other aspects of Old First programs or buildings is that they experience all change as loss. Sometimes it is loss, but even when change is growth, it is experienced as loss. That is a fundamental reality underlying pastoral care.

For these reasons, unlocking memories is a way of affirming people and their church. Pastors should not move in to change Old Firsts. Radical amputations of traditional programs, budgets, and buildings are seldom helpful or necessary early in one's pastorate. Recovery of the historic vision and the affirmation of the great acts of God's people in the past, together with the creative celebration of them in the present will eventually produce a congregational climate where expective change can and will take place. People who have no memories can set no goals. The way forward is first a creative look back.

Chapter 2
Securing the Vantage Point

Since all ministry involves serving people in their environment, one cannot think of ministry without thinking of context. All ministry occurs within a context. What do we mean by that? Many people feel that it is the place wherever human action occurs, and to a certain extent this is obviously true. However, this chapter suggests that context is more than simply the place where action occurs. Equally important are those events and occurrences that have taken place in the past. Contexts are in a real sense consequences—environmental, economic, and political consequences of historical forces. Context is the residue of the past experienced in the present.

There was a time in the past when the four major environments (rural, town, suburb, and city) had distinctive dynamics, lifestyles, and subcultures. In the United States those distinctions are becoming increasingly fewer and farther between.

Reflection upon the Old First cases reveals that from the very earliest days there were common themes rooted in common theological commitments. Some of the earliest rural churches in what is today generally considered a bastion of conservatism were congregations involved in the Underground Railroad in southern Ohio. Salvation and social justice were part of the same gospel commitments in those days.

While at the time of the War of Independence the American colonies had as many as twenty communities with populations in excess of three thousand people, colonial America was largely rural. Ninety-five percent lived in rural areas. Now America is largely urban, with over 90 percent of Americans living in cities as of 1990. However, despite the large proportion of Americans who are urban dwellers, many still prefer the smaller scale of village or rural life.

There are many distinct contrasts between village or rural life as it existed during the early years of the planting of Old First churches and present rural life. The first distinction has to do with the level of permanence of the people in the rural setting or, to put it another way, the depth of the roots people have in that setting. Before the advent of the automobile, people who lived in a rural setting rarely traveled more than fifty miles from their home; actual relocation, except in times of calamity, was even more unusual. With the prevalence of the automobile, mobility among American families became a distinct way of life. The average family is likely to be relocated because of the career demands of the principal wage earner in the family. Increased mobility has replaced the permanence in rural life, thereby destroying an unshakable bond between land and people.

Another distinction between rural life of an earlier period and the present time is the nature of work of the people. In earlier times, village and rural dwellers were largely farmers and craftsmen. In today's setting, the proportion of farmers has radically diminished. The persons who choose to live in a rural setting may be professionals, executives, or white-collar employees of a local corporation or factory. In a sense, then, given the context of mobility, life in a rural or village setting is now a matter of *choice,* not obligation as was the case in former times. The relative calm of rural life as compared to the bustle of urban life has a certain attraction for some people; the undisturbed environment and countryside has an inescapable charm for others. The point here is that for a large and growing segment of the work force, the decision to live in a rural or village setting is a matter of quality of life—not economics.

A third distinction is the general economic structure of rural life. Because the corporation now has become so embedded in American life, there is a distinct relationship between the power of the corporation and the changed economic structure of village life. The day has gone when the influence of a corporation was limited to a local setting or even the borderline of a state. The power of corporations now extends beyond state borders, through regions, across the nation, and often, throughout the world. The presumed autonomy of village life or the independence of rural life has been no match for the power of a corporate giant. The same ways in which corporations wield power in the cities are now seen in the rural setting. The intense trading in pork belly futures on the Chicago Stock Market has a direct effect on the ability of a farmer in rural Ohio to meet the mortgage payments on a farm which may have been in the family for generations. This says that the same forces which are so much a part of our urbanized American lifestyle have come to have a distinct influence on rural and village life. There can be no escape from such effects, despite the attempts of some to seek the pastures of calm which presumably await them beyond the city limits.

Several churches in our study have roots in rural life which indeed go back to the early days of the Republic. However, as we have noted earlier, there are distinct changes in the way of life as it exists now and as it existed at an earlier point in time. The Whitesboro Baptist Church is located in the village of Whitesboro, New York, an area adjacent to Utica, New York. The village, founded in 1784, was the fashionable and affluent suburb where generations of Utica residents spent their summers. While Whitesboro has not experienced all of the turmoil of deterioration characteristic of many urbanized suburbs, it is no longer the affluent suburb it was in the past. A high proportion of its residents are elderly, and a disproportionate number of them are in their eighties and nineties.

At the same time, many younger families have moved into the area, including the neighborhood immediately surrounding the church. However, in terms of overall church membership, activity, and wealth, all of the Protestant churches in the village are dwarfed by the two large Roman Catholic parishes. Overall, the socioeconomic structure of Whitesboro has changed. No longer exclusively white Anglo-Saxon Protestant, no longer exclusively middle class, the village is still regarded by most people as a good place to live. Many of its large old homes, especially along the older streets, are now multiple dwelling units, and their inhabitants may tend to be more transient. Urbanization has descended upon Whitesboro.

While the incursion of urbanization has been relatively kind to Whitesboro and the Whitesboro Church, it has taken a greater toll on the village of Ossining, New York, where the First Baptist Church seeks to rejuvenate itself after a period of decline. Because First Baptist Church of Ossining is situated squarely in the center of the village, it experienced all of the effects of the neighborhood deterioration that took place in the 1960s and the early 1970s. In the early to middle 1970s the church was facing extinction or the possibility of being forced into a yoked fellowship with another congregation. Many of the parishioners were ready to close the doors because attendance was dwindling and there was a clear financial crisis. In 1974 the worship attendance was about sixty-five and the budget was thirty-thousand dollars. Situated in the middle of a blighted area, the church was the neighbor of persons who were either on welfare or belonged to the class of the "working poor." By this time there were few affluent members of the church. However, while urbanization caused much deterioration in Ossining, the political aspects of a mobilized urban consciousness, exemplified by a particularly successful urban renewal project and vigorous pastoral and lay leadership of the church, has produced extraordinary changes in the last decade. A new spirit has been kindled in the body of believers on the corners of South Highland Avenue, Church Street, and Main Street in Ossining.

Average attendance at worship services is now between 140 and 150, and the annual budget has increased more than 100 percent to eighty thousand dollars in 1974. The debilitating and inexorable march of urbanization into the formerly stable village of Ossining appears to have been successfully met by the inspired will of Old First of Ossining.

Another context that has evolved relative to the ministry of Old First churches is the peculiarly American phenomenon of the small town. Towns, especially Midwestern towns, evolved and proliferated wherever the "rivers met the railroads" as America expanded westward. Rockford, Illinois, for example, was the ford on the Rock River. Towns thus share with cities an economic motive: they were formed to respond to the trading impulses of early pioneers and to the economic needs of settlers.

However, along with the economic impulse of the town there were certain social and political motives. County seat towns formed so that people could travel to their county seats within a half day's ride and reach home again for the evening chores. The impulse among frontier settlers to congregate for social functions, to legislate laws to resolve conflict, and to regulate relations among commercial enterprises also occasioned the rise of towns. Towns became the county seats, state capitols, and regional trading centers which would bring persons from the rural areas to conduct business, inquire into the legal aspects of life, and generally maintain social exchange with others.

The town in nineteenth and early twentieth-century America assumed a distinct cultural mode as well as an economic thrust. The town represented continuity and stability; the citizens of the town shared a common memory of events, personalities, and natural calamities which gave a distinct personality to that place. There was a corporate understanding of "us" as opposed to any "them" who might happen to be strangers. The members of the Hamilton Square Baptist Church of Hamilton Township, New Jersey, have a memory of the agrarian roots of the township. The memory which defines the identity of the members was and still is to a certain extent that of large farming families which had owned nearby farms for generations. Juxtaposed to this memory has been the changes which industrialization brought after the 1950s and the attendant tendency of blue-collar families to move to a suburban ring around the township. Such families were determined to share in the upward mobility that the American Dream symbolized. Expectedly, the corporate memory of the "we" was at odds with the rather unfocused identity of the "they." There is a conflict between the world view of the town and the world view of the surrounding suburb. The town shares a corporate memory which is oriented to the past while the suburban world view is oriented to the future—a life of eternally hoped-for possibilities. For the church in Hamilton the "mix of the past and present has been oftentimes difficult…, but it has attempted to be honest and open with such issues as race, war and peace, and reconciliation in the midst of diversity."[1]

Throughout human history at least two cultural forces have been associated with the rise of cities and the urban environment: the establishment of a sense of civilization, often among culturally diverse peoples; and the growth of diversified market activity. These two phenomena were no less important in the emergence of cities during the very early years of the American experience. The settlers of North America in the early seventeenth century, both voluntary settlers who left Europe and elsewhere and involuntary settlers who were forcibly taken from the African continent, sought new beginnings in the New World with memories of the Old World. These memories included those of settlements, towns, and cities, of London and Mali, Amsterdam and Songhay, Paris and Ashanti. These diverse peoples then set about the task of creating the new with the memory of the old. The second great cultural phenomenon that gives rise to cities—the market impulse—has been very much a part of the early cities of America, especially the "Big Three"—New

York, Philadelphia, and Boston. By virtue of having developed deep water harbors, these cities had relatively easy access to the money and commodity markets of Europe. Other inland cities likewise grew in proportion to their commercial importance during the early years of the Republic. Yet despite all of these developments, urban expansion in the nation as a whole was very, very slow. By the end of the eighteenth century still only 10 percent of all of the American people could be considered urban dwellers.

Contrasted to this rather sluggish rate of urban growth in the latter years of the eighteenth century was the explosive growth patterns which began during the third decade of the nineteenth century. Beginning in the 1820s the United States began to experience a phenomenal rate of growth in its cities. Several factors accounted for this growth, chief among them being the surge of population moving westward after the War of 1812 and the development of faster and more efficient transportation systems, notably canals and railroads. Another factor was the infusion into the general population of a great number of immigrants from Ireland, Eastern Europe, and Russia. The vast proportion of these immigrants remained close to their disembarkation sites, principally New York City. Other immigrants pushed into the heartland of the nation. Up until the Civil War era, the Midwest region was settling from the bottom up along the river systems. Agrarian peoples generally came west through the Cumberland Gap, producing a rural subculture some characterize as the "Bible Belt" over a large area of the country.

By 1870 there was an interdependent network of sizable cities stretching from coast to coast which played an important role in organizing the national economy. Urbanism was indeed beginning to characterize a great part of "the American way of life." In a way, urbanism was the result of the notion of American "manifest destiny" channeled into industrial might. Well before Calvin Coolidge declared that the business of America was business, commentators on the American scene in the 1870s and thereafter could point to a correlation between the strength of the American economic structure and the growth of cities. In 1866 one writer for *The Nation* observed that in the bustling economy and lifestyle of the cities one could find "the real national life."[2] Yet there was an ambivalence about this emerging form of national life. While many could appreciate cities for their cultural, educational, and economic offerings, many could also see immanent decay in the form of congested housing, crime, and political corruption. The ambivalence many must still feel in attempting to come to terms with the meaning of the city points to the fact that there is a fundamental paradox at the heart of the city. While the city represented the full flowering of liberation from the constraints of the traditional society and village life, it also contained the seeds for human misery. Traditional village societies, characterized by close ethnic, face-to-face relationships, could provide a bulwark against spiritual uncertainty and emotional isolation. The price one paid, however, was a rather humdrum and tedious life, one not open to new ideas or to new people. By contrast the city offered ethnic diversity and exposure to the ferment of human creativity, new ideas, and new notions. Here in the city, however, the price one paid could be the cold impersonality that strangers often experience when they encounter new places or faces.

A second and related paradox lies at the heart of the city. If the first paradox has to do with the structure of the city, which at the same time offers freedom *and* bondage, hope *and* despair, the second paradox has to do with the individual's search for meaning and fulfillment. It should always be remembered that cities were perhaps the first human settlements where diversity was tolerated and encouraged. Individual initiative could be played out on the stage of a relatively open society, at least when compared with traditional or folk society. Cities provided the individual with a measure of freedom which could never be hoped for in the constraints of traditional society.

What is paradoxical is that this ethos of the city—allowing for individualism and individual fulfillment—also helps create the very conditions in which the individual feels helpless in the midst of our mass consumer society. Without the power of individual initiative and the gathering of diverse peoples and the markets they provided, it is doubtful that the capitalist political economy ever would have emerged in its modern form. Yet the city in its present form seems to have become the very place in our society where countless persons have given up attempting to find the dream of individual fulfillment. Such persons now claim the attention of Old Firsts.

The urban Old Firsts ministering to industrializing centers have responded by institutionalizing their ministries to meet the widening range of human needs present in those environments. Despite the suspicions and divisions that eventually rocked the denominations with Old Firsts, a profound commonality can be observed. Each congregation in substance and style was seeking to respond faithfully to increasingly diverse environments. It is in the best interest of denominations to own that fact, and it is necessary if reconciliation is to occur.

The suburb was the latest of the four environments to emerge. In its earliest days it probably represented the same threat to the city that the county seat town did to the rural areas. Later the suburbs came to symbolize the "white-flight/white fright" syndrome as the cities, towns, and rural areas experienced a common reality: vast populations left them for the suburbs.

Contemporary Dynamics and Environmental Changes

When President Jimmy Carter announced the embargo on wheat sales to Russia, every farmer learned that rural American individualism and freedom no longer existed. Farmers in their petrochemical-dependent, stereo-equipped tractors discovered that they were part of an industrialized assembly line called "the futures market" of the grain exchanges. Now in the late twentieth century nearly every rural community experiences the pain of a vise-like matrix. In reality the urban poor and farmers—the new rural poor—are allies. This has profound implications for the Old Firsts in both environments.

Meanwhile the town is changing just as dramatically. The basic elements of old small towns are still largely visible.

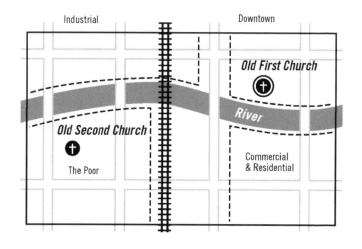

DIAGRAM A

The ethos of the old town is corporate: people say "we." It is memory oriented; persons are known by their family and location. Church and cemetery are central to social maps.

Today we see many changes in these historic patterns. A ring of new housing has emerged around the old towns which have incorporated previously rural spaces and zoned them for commercial use or light industry in an expanded expressway culture. So the new town realities include:

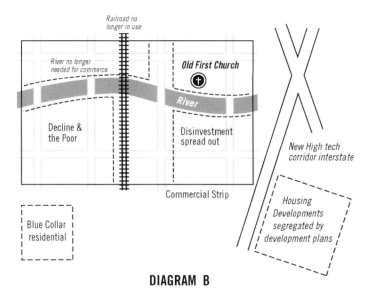

DIAGRAM B

The outer ring contains as many people as the inner ring, but those in the outer ring are individualistic in orientation (I versus we), future-oriented, and known by their vocational identities rather than by family and place. Pluralism has become the norm in the small towns, and Old Firsts are caught in the conflict of two very different realities. Many Old Firsts move to the outer ring and recontextualize; others stay and eventually die along with the mom and pop hardware stores and locally owned banks. Still others regionalize, branch out, pluralize their programs, find new identities and styles, and grow. Those who stay alive and stay downtown find themselves in declining socioeconomic realities, sharing that same historic space with all sorts of new varieties of sect and church.

Until recently the American suburbs were exempt, but now almost every problem that was called "urban" can be found there also. Their streets and water systems are aging. Massive school commitments are built on declining property tax bases and declining populations, with little history of commitment to community. Consumerism and narcissism have proved false gods for families who sought these havens or promised lands. Migrant or relocated Old Firsts probably will find that these suburbs are less *the escape* from the big bad cities than the *extensions* of them. Increasingly, there is no such place as "away." Contextual analysis produces some surprises for many. The historic or classically differentiated environments are changing. The Old Firsts within them have increasingly changed environments which are radically different from environments of the past.

Community Entry and Discovery Processes

In the previous chapter we suggested that historical analysis and reflection can free up memories and unleash new energies and creativity for pastors and congregations. The same thing can be said about community analysis and reflection. Some old congregations have lost touch with new realities. Programmatic rigidity becomes the compensation for the good old days of yore. In each environment the leadership core generally continues to call pastors who will affirm the old images, symbols, and behavior patterns. Theology and program fuse. Congregational behavior systems prop up the belief systems. The name of this Old First is "Legion" and we have all been in the midst of it.

Generally speaking, there are two ways to study a community: formally and informally. The formal study entails going to libraries and reading the histories, studies, and lore of the community. A sophisticated approach might involve census track analysis and population pyramids that graphically describe what is changing in social or economic terms. Precision can be added to such a study by interview guides and opinion samples.

Far better for the Old First is the informal or network approach to the community study process. While an Old First church may have one committee or task force studying the history, as suggested in the previous chapter, they can have a second one researching the community. They might divide into five sub-teams and make visits and have each group explore the dynamics or changes in an area. The teams would then return to the church and ask, "What are the implications of this information for Old First?" The primary advantage of an informal networking approach is that you learn not only the issues, but the people and the processes of the community as well. You find the services that exist and have some idea of what is still needed to "scratch the people where they really itch" in the name of Jesus.

Here are some of the categories under which you may find valuable community information:

1. *Politics*
   Village and county agencies
   Political organizations and activities
   Non-partisan community organizations (leagues,
      councils, commissions, committees, and so forth)
   Events, issues, personalities, census data
   Strategies for involvement and mobilization
   Calendars, election districts, and so forth
   Histories, trends and projections, plans

2. *Economics*
   Commercial institutions (banks, savings and loans,
      and so forth)
   Manufacturing
   Insurance
   Retail organizations
   Realtors and housing
   International business
   State offices
   Social Security, Internal Revenue
   Issues, events, personalities, service clubs
   Plans, zoning, resources

3. *Education*
   Preschool
   Elementary, secondary
   Special education
   Other schools
   Other educational agencies, libraries, and so forth
   Cultural institutions: art centers, concerts, theaters, and so forth
   Service clubs
   Issues, events, personalities
   Trends and projections

4. *Health and Welfare*
   Hospitals, clinics, and other institutions
   Group homes
   Special programs for the needy, elderly, retarded, and others
   Police, jails, public safety
   Scouts, youth organizations
   Parks and recreation
   Special services: counseling, crisis, emergencies, and so forth
   Issues, events, personalities, trends, projections

5. *Church and Religion*
   Churches, pastors, denominations, programs, census
   Other ministries that are church- or parachurch-based
   Special committees that may relate to areas
   Descriptions of church topologies and assessments
   Issues, events, personalities, trends, or projections

Pastors can become involved in the community if they make it a major commitment (which the authors think it should be) or part of the "big five" duties:

- Preaching
- Teaching
- Caring
- Administrating
- Networking

Prayer and study infuses all of these. One day a week or its equivalent should be set aside for pastoral networking. Three rounds of community visits are immediately obvious.

First, visit other churches. You may begin your visit by saying, "I am the pastor of _____(Old First) Baptist Church. I am quite new in the community and I need your help. Can you tell me the most important lesson you have learned about being a pastor in this community since you have begun?" Notice that this kind of approach is neutral and nonthreatening. Amazing things can happen as you invite your colleagues to teach you lessons they have learned—regardless of the denominational or theological labels.

A second round of pastoral visits can include the executives and staffs of community social agencies, which would include schools, police, and the Social Security office. Many of these groups have broader grass roots constituencies than the churches in those same communities. They can tell pastors a great deal about problems facing families and individuals of the community.

The final round of visits can include the local business establishments—from the flower shop and café to the factories. A great deal can be learned from these conversations about changing patterns. One legacy will be a community network that knows the pastor's concerns and commitments. This information can have extraordinary significance for informing and defining the local church's priorities as it seeks to shape its mission in that community.

It should become obvious what services are being delivered and who is being served. Put another way, it should become obvious who the unreached people are: those untouched by any church, and those who have never heard the Good News of Jesus Christ.

Pastors who network their communities, especially in the first year of a pastorate, may end up knowing that community better than any other person. This upfront investment of time should pay rich dividends later and provide the opportunity to help people with multiplied options and resources already cataloged. Busy pastors can cut through a great deal of red tape in emergencies through the prior investment in relationships.

Notice, especially in the previous sentence, the phrase "investment in relationships." This is very different from another well-known pattern we might call "consumer of relationships" or resources. It is very important that pastors and congregations invest and serve as well as take from their environments. One might think this should go without saying, but many old churches may be presuming that enormous historic goodwill exists in their community that in reality may not exist anymore in our increasingly secular society. Some neighborhoods may resent the influx of commuters, congestion, and noise. Rising concerns about church tax exemptions and the well-publicized extravagance of certain television ministries may have served to erode the historic goodwill toward Old First. The problem of alienation in the neighborhoods may have been inadvertently exacerbated in recent years by new fences, walls, gates, and lock systems. In fact, a parking lot of non-local cars, the dress, fashions, color, language, and worship styles of churchgoers often become sentient carriers of a behavior system that communicates a loud and clear "stay away" signal to the community. The *belief system* of the church may not have changed. The pastor may still be preaching "you all come to Jesus!" but the *behavior system* of the congregation can be communicating an intent to screen those who join. These realities can be subtle and undetected by the members until the pathology of communicating church alienation becomes the overpowering reality.

Some Contextual Reflections

While there are numerous exceptions to any generalization, the burden of this chapter is to show that despite the disparities and uniqueness of Old First environments in the past, the urban/rural gaps have narrowed. While there are differences still between rural and urban environments, the differences are of degree and not primarily of substance. Cities are the historic engines of cultural and economic change for a variety of reasons. The city, like time-lapse photography, shows change and exposes the dynamics of that change. It becomes clear that we should study ministry in large cities—not to see how unique or different it is—but so it can show us where the whole country is moving or will be twenty years hence. We can see that the structured injustices that produced structured poverty and the widening disparities between the haves and the have-nots that characterized urban life are also realities in rural life. In fact, we can argue that we should study ministry in urban contexts for the same reasons we study counseling in psychiatric settings—not because those patients are so different from us, but because the behaviors we all possess (and usually hide well) are much more visible there and therefore easier to diagnose.

At the very least then, new dialogue and alliances between pastors of old churches, both urban and rural, ought to emerge at this time. No longer should the successful or the unsuccessful models of Old First renewal be dismissed just because they came from historically different environments. There is a great deal that any of the churches can learn from the others despite age, racial composition, or diversity of population.

It should also be obvious that seminaries cannot continue to teach theology as though it was environmentally neutral material. The sound exegesis of the Word requires the acquisition of basic tools, like biblical languages, hermeneutics, and interpretation skills, sharpened by studies in church history and social ethics. Likewise the exegesis of environments requires a tool kit for neighborhood analysis, especially the vision to see what is taking place and the imagination that the Holy Spirit gives, making creative sensitivities and possibilities a reality for the church.

No doubt there are some neighborhoods that have been so rezoned or disinvested that there are no longer any people, but those situations are probably far fewer than first imagined. Old Firsts were those churches that celebrated God's transcendence over local structures. Old Firsts were those who proclaimed the creative as well as redemptive mandates of God. They therefore possess theological resources for bankrupt communities—resources other churches can only dream about. We now turn to the task of recovery of that theological vision.

Chapter 3
Theological Foundations and Practice

Rabbi Robert Gordis, in his remarkable commentary on the Hebrew text of Ecclesiastes called *Koheleth: The Man and His World: A Study of Ecclesiastes*,[1] suggests that the Bible (in this case the Old Testament) or the "divine library," has several theological world views. If you were to meet an old priest on the streets of ancient Jerusalem and ask him, "When are the 'good old days'?" he would tell you they were back in the wilderness when the memory of God's miracles of deliverance was very fresh and Moses was the leader. There is, suggests Gordis, a memory tradition in which the eyes of God's people are fixed on the great acts of God in the past and they are thus backing into the future.

If you continued down the street and met an old prophet and asked, "When are the 'good old days'?" you would be told they are in the future when the Messiah will come and when justice will reign on the earth. There is, suggests Gordis, a futuristic perspective in the literature of the divine library.

Should you continue down the ancient street and encounter a Hebrew sage or poet and ask, "When are the 'good old days'?" he would shrug his shoulders, throw up his hands and say something like, "Enjoy! Enjoy! It will never get better. It will never be worse!" There is, Gordis continues, a theology of the meantime in the poetical literature of the divine library; the meantime is between the great acts of God in the past and the great acts of God in the future. The exiles who returned to Jerusalem were called upon to rebuild a city, a culture, and the faith of a people who saw all around them the reminders of their great past. The wisdom tradition of poetry and practical theology developed precisely in this matrix and under those dynamics.

If one attempted to discern a prominent theological theme that permeates the history of the Old First experience and the reflection on the contemporary Old First situation, surely that one theme would be the creative balance between the transcendence and the immanence of God. The Almighty is viewed and understood as *over* all but at the same time disclosed in and *through* the human condition. As the Gordis story suggests, the transcendence of God is understood in the temporal sphere: past, present, and future form a unified whole in God. Yet the significance of the remembered past and the expected future are experienced and given vitality in the present.

God is Creator, Redeemer, and Lord of all. The ever-present and creative tension between transcendence and immanence helps explain why the historic Old First would place so much emphasis on the *creative* aspects of community life and building, on the ceaseless attempts at *redeeming* people and places, and a commitment to including persons of all ethnic, age, and class distinctions. Thus there is fidelity to the notions of *creation, redemption,* and *inclusiveness* in the theological orientation of the Old First tradition. We will now turn to a more detailed discussion of these themes within the context of the Old First experience.

Since Old First people were imbued with a sense of history, they understood the importance of a good beginning. Just as God uses history as the medium for self-disclosure, God's people act out their fidelity to the Almighty within history. Woven into the historic fabric of Old Firsts are the threads of a definite theological orientation which attests to this assertion. The case studies of Old Firsts delight in reporting that these congregations usually helped create the settlement from which the town or city would emerge generations later.

Obed Denham, the fierce opponent of slavery, was one of the founders of the Bethel Baptist Church of Bethel, Ohio, chartered in 1798. It is interesting to note that while the settlement he planted nearby in 1796 was named Plainfield, the same name of the place he left in New Jersey, the settlement was commonly called Denhamstown.[2] Baptists were a part of the beginning years of Geneva, New York, when they joined others who were attracted to the opening of tracts of land known as the Holland Purchase.[3] Such attraction was enhanced by the liberal inducements made by land companies which offered free land for schools and churches. The first settlers in Hamilton, New York, originally called Payne's Settlement, were outstanding Baptist laypersons from Dutchess County, New York, led by Samuel Payne in 1794. A year later he sent for his brother, Elisha, who brought his family and several others. In 1796 the Paynes and other committed Baptists founded the First Baptist Church of Hamilton.[4] The spiritual descendants of the founders of the Pine City Baptist Church of Pine City, New York, the first Baptist church to be founded in that area, celebrate the link between the impulse to settle the wilderness and the desire and will to found a church. Perhaps no more poignant description of the intense energy of the settlers could be provided than the following account of the earliest days of Pine City:

> The first to arrive usually settled near the junction of a main stream and a river. Those who came later followed the stream up various valleys to points where smaller streams joined. These streams and their immediate surroundings provided the water, fish, and wild game necessary for survival. One stream the settlers followed was Seeley Creek, and, as we know today, settlements developed at the junction of Seeley Creek and smaller tributaries—namely, South Creek (Bulkhead), Dry Run (Pine City), Bird Creek (Webb Mills), Mudlick (Sagetown) and Seeley Creek (Seeley Creek).
>
> Families usually came in early spring, so that enough time would be available to clear the land and get in a small

crop, planted to provide food for the coming winter. Many families came through the Pine City area by oxcart. The area was covered by a stand of pine and hemlock so dense that there was only room for the oxcarts to pass without further clearing. They had to go farther up the valley, beyond the heavy pine, to a higher elevation, where the hard woods grew less dense, in order to find land suitable for a crop and easier to clear in the short time.

Implicit in the role of the settler was the sense that order should drive out chaos, that a design for life should fill the vacuum which a non-structured environment offered. These settlers and founders of Old Firsts willingly took on the roles of prophets and moral guides for the whole community, thus making them much more catholic in their perspective than the churches with no social conscience that we see in many settings today. Having been a part of the creative force which brought communities into being, they did not shirk the responsibility inherent in their power nor flee from the burden that went along with that power.

Because Old First settlers answered the call from God to be a part of the creative force in founding and building communities, they were also imbued with a will to be alert to the redemptive possibilities of creation in general and of their own particular communities in specific. The redemption theology of Old Firsts recognized the power inherent in the transcendence of God seen in the valleys, hills, and rivers that wound through settlements. In later years, the transcendence of God was seen in neighborhoods that became run down and streets filled with potholes. God was there and everywhere and bade the faithful to be vigilant to the task of redeeming humanity and humanity's environment. Redemption theology demands that we not abandon environments and throw away neighborhoods just because banks discourage mortgage loans in "undesirable areas" or politicians gerrymander districts into powerlessness.

The theological orientation of Old Firsts also reminds us of the plurality of world views present in the Bible. Pastors meet three groups in their congregations: those who live in the past, those who live for the future, and others who live day by day. Preaching should not neglect this true pluralism. An informed biblical world view must celebrate the God who was, is, and is to come. To proclaim that, we must behave with integrity even when the socioeconomic signs and culture point in different directions. Christians must see data differently.

Like the Reformers, we struggle to hold together creation theology (that which God is doing in the environment of the world) and redemption theology (that which God is doing in the unique mission of the church) and keep them in tension.

Old Firsts blended the two ideas by developing a cohesive mission. In their earliest days Old Firsts had a sanctuary, a single pastor, and little else. How shall we interpret this pattern today? Perhaps Old Firsts did not run specialized programs in their earliest years because they saw the church and its environment as a whole or as a seamless garment. The garment fit comfortably because these churches made no distinction between the sacred and the secular, between clean and unclean, between that which was considered appropriate for church business and that which was not. As long as the welfare of women, men, families, and the environment was at stake, Old Firsts considered any issue appropriate for their attention.

Historically, however, Old Firsts were the counterpoint to an exclusivistic religion, a purely privatistic faith. The religion of Old Firsts affirmed the aspirations of all of the people God had gathered into a flock whose faith was articulated in sermons, lifestyles, architecture, worship, and programs. All of these were designed to proclaim that God was Lord of the whole earth and everything within it. The church was built often as a communal effort and topped off physically and symbolically by the steeple, which attested to the fact that here were *God's* people—not a mere collection of individuals. Sermons, true to the Reformation impulse, were the high point of the worship service—the time of sharing God's Word with people. It is true that Old Firsts did not advocate a primitive communalism, but they did frown on any member so imbued with his or her own concern to the exclusion of concern for others. To be effective signs and agents of God's kingdom, something theologically akin to Old First is needed today, perhaps more than ever, to check the social narcissism rampant in American culture and congregations.

The open and inclusive spirit of Old Firsts extended to the whole community full of sinners and those sinned against. They knew that the whole creation agonized under the travail of sin. While they recognized the personal traumas caused by sin and the forgivability of sin, they also saw a bigger picture that included the artifacts of sin or structures of corporate evil and injustice created by sinful persons. They recognized the sinners, but they also recognized that many of them were at the same time the "sinned against."

The inclusivism of Old Firsts also extended to generations of families. The communities that founded Old First churches understood that the young and the old were equally important in the chain of being. English philosopher John Ruskin observed that society was a pact between the living, the dead, and the unborn. So too Old Firsts understood the importance of each generation. The symbolic tie with the past generations was made through the consecration and devout maintenance of cemeteries next to Old First churches. In reviewing its history, the First Baptist Church of Schenectady, New York, noted that the first key decision of the congregation after gathering together in 1822 was to secure a plot of land for a burial ground in 1824.[6] Devoutly maintained by the living, the cemeteries contained the remains of the saints of those churches—the witness to a Bethel (see Genesis 35:15). The cemetery represented the special love God had for that place, a redemptive covenant of sealed hope. In other words, Old Firsts embodied a holistic view that embraced life and death, individuals and institutions, wealth and poverty, the past and the future. God was incarnate in that community, and Old Firsts developed a highly stylized liturgical form in worship to celebrate that fact. They affirmed the uplifting majesty of a holy and righteous God.

Old Firsts embodied an incarnational theology that was demonstrated in their holistic and inclusive perspective on generations and community and their redemptive concern for the environment.

In Old Firsts as in other structures, when the Holy Spirit chooses to incarnate in the life and world of community leaders, the gospel message may take the shape and values of the target audience. Our unique aesthetic tastes or personal spiritual diets are not the primary issues in discussions like this. The functions of every biblically responsible congregation may be the same, but the *forms* their programs take must be different in every time and place to be faithful to the gospel and to Christ's model.

Theology really does make a difference in one's world view, and that in turn informs a ministry perspective. At this point in our nation's history, the United States is debating the relative openness of our borders. We are taking in multiethnic populations from every part of God's earth. Why, we might ask from the theological perspective, is God bringing all these people to us, if it is not for ultimate spiritually significant purposes, i.e., to renew our churches and mission agencies and to assist us in the two-thousand-year task of discipling the nations for our Lord?

Readers of Ezekiel 16, a classic biblical passage for developing an urban theology, will notice that as God looks at cities, the ethnicity and environment flow together in a kind of choreography of nations, people, and cities. In the book of Obadiah, Jacob and Esau have become occupants of rival cities on rival mountains. In this contest the brutal contemporary war and international politics of Edom are condemned as though their wars were the continued struggle between two brothers. Think about how God views nations today.

Old Firsts have traditionally lifted up these global issues of our faith. They look at local persons and see cosmic issues at stake. Every community needs some church (an Old First or another) to raise the global consciousness questions and the transnational significance of our faith. In the past, Old Firsts had huge foreign mission budgets. In fact, the influence of these old churches led to the creation of many large mission structures we still celebrate.

Now that cities and even rural communities are becoming racially and linguistically more pluralistic, many American Christians have become nervous about the fact that 87 percent of the world is yellow, brown, and black and that our country is beginning to reflect those realities. In fact, many local churches are resegregating themselves to maintain the growth of persons who are just like themselves. There are some strategic advantages to segmenting the environment for evangelistic purposes, but the very building of the walls between social groups in our own day tends to narrow the gospel and splinter God's kingdom.

Old Firsts have historically sensitive eyes that regard Belfast, Beirut, Capetown, Los Angeles, or Miami as sisters as were Jerusalem, Samaria, and Sodom in Ezekiel 16. This global perspective on God's creation and God's international redemption plan leads to different sensitivities to new language groups who reside in the community. Old Firsts have provided spaces and programs for very diverse groups of strangers and exiles. While Old Firsts have been strongly nationalistic over the years, they also have given witness to the international character of the gospel in ways beyond the abilities of other kinds of churches. Again, this is a theological perspective on God and the world that is urgently needed in the center of every American community. Under the pressure of unemployment or other traumas, foreigners become the scapegoats of Christians who can be seen wrapping their gospel in the flag of the nation or living out their frustrations against other nations with their "Buy American" campaigns. While we can all appreciate the anger and frustration of our neighbors, Old Firsts ought not succumb to harangues or sermons that bless such behaviors.

In remaining faithful to their unique calling, Old Firsts are not just local churches in the communities that function like clubhouses for members. Rather, they are of and for the community as a whole.

The parallel critique of Old Firsts is that they often seem to succumb to the temptation to cavort with social harlots and defer to the rich and powerful establishment. No doubt this has happened far too often in the past, and as a result the uncompromising message of the gospel has been blunted or watered down. Bowing to prestige is always a threat to our incarnational witness for Christ. Avoiding that tendency requires vigilant accountability to the larger body of the church. Granted, some Old Firsts mistook their special mission assignment of "chosenness" for "favoriteness," assuming they were better than other churches and really did not need them. However, we all know missionaries who communicate their superiority to the rest of us and make ordinary church members feel like second-class Christians. However, we cannot use that fact to deny the validity of the call of mission work. Rather we must insist that Old Firsts adhere to their unique servant role. It is our gift, our voice, our witness to cultural groups we would not ordinarily reach. Old First is a legitimate mission!

As one of their priestly functions, Old Firsts must point out pathology in community systems. Old Firsts must witness to God's judgment and call the system to accountability and change. People repent, but that is not enough. Old Firsts need to challenge people like Zacchaeus not only to change their personal behavior, but also to rectify the policies they are implementing. The church must strive for peace with justice—not just keeping the peace. Old Firsts have kingly roles as stewards of power to bring about wise rule and wise stewardship of all of God's resources. The church needs to be the conscience of the cities when it comes to an environmental imperative. The cities have no right to pollute or waste God's water or the earth that God has created. Old Firsts have traditionally watched over God's creation agendas. Is that role needed less today?

Faithful to Old Testament mandates, Old Firsts exist to challenge Christian Josephs to design new seven-year plans for budget deficits and surpluses, and to feed hungry nations while working for pagan Pharaohs. Old Firsts are needed today to help migrant workers like Daniel sort out issues of faith and culture in the modern world; to teach the new arrivals and emerging leaders how to master Nebuchadnezzar's knowledge while rejecting his lifestyle. Old Firsts are needed today to help the creative, internationally involved Nehemiahs of our day to get their grants and design urban development programs for cities in ruin. Who will counsel these leaders on these mission agendas if not today's revitalized Old First churches? A vital Old First senses God's transcendence on the one hand and global awareness on the other andis not intimidated.

Today's Old First can sort through the personal dilemma of a Queen Esther with all the attendant spiritual ambiguities of her life in the harem. While lay theological reflection could have rendered her a passive victim, Old Firsts would see theologically that God can use the personal for redemptive purposes (see Esther 4:14). Old First pastors have Mordecai's role of theological reflector for people of power caught in life's dramatic ambiguities.

The pastors of Old First churches reflect on international migrants like Onesimus who flee from economic bondage in underdeveloped countries only to get lost in the multiethnic urban crowds of advanced countries. Old Firsts say to the Philemons of our day that "perhaps" God has larger purposes in what has happened. Who will declare these aspects of God's activities if those who run the towns, cities, and nations are not within the earshot of the pulpits of Old First churches? Surely if the Old First pulpit did not exist we would have to invent it to be faithful to the whole counsel of God, especially in our day.

The Old First of today—so unlike the powerful Old First of the past—faces a future which may hold out the promise of renewal, but often is confronted with a present that appears devoid of hope. Discernment of the will of God in historic events, even dire and seemingly hopeless events, forces all who love Old First to ask if there is any hint of providence in this particular predicament. We conclude the chapter with some reflections on this question.

Concerning the theological appropriation of time and history Old Firsts need the practical theology of the wisdom tradition of ancient Israel when the temptation comes to live on nostalgic memories or apocalyptic dreams. Neither of these, in and of themselves, addresses the realities of the situation at hand. At the same time there is the opposite danger of living so exclusively for and in the present that the great acts of God—both past and future— are denied.

On a purely intellectual level it is relatively easy for the people of Old First churches to affirm the theological importance of the past, present, and future. Yet in its current predicament they must categorically deny that seeking refuge in purely intellectual concepts is desirable or even possible. The predicament demands a "flesh and blood" appropriation of a heavenly ideal. The inescapable mandate confronting Old Firsts is that they be the organizations in the contemporary environment that take seriously the rather obvious implication that we accept the elderly and the young as equal members of the Christian community. Acceptance, often-times voiced too hastily and glibly, is not enough! The God of history points out that the crucial importance of elders is their position as repositories of what God has done in some lives in the past. Such persons are therefore living testimonies to what God has done in that community.

There may be clear sociological signals of God at work in this mandate to become a truly multigenerational community. These signals may be seen in the transformation of the American family. After World War II the concept of the nuclear family reached its ascendancy in American society. This concept vaunted the ideal of two parents, one girl, and one boy all living in a single family dwelling in the suburbs, supported by the single income of the father. Dislocations in the American economy, however, have meant that families must now depend on two wage earners. More than 80 percent of female spouses in the country now are employed outside of the home in some capacity. At the same time changes in the economy have taken their toll on the elderly, sending many of them into poverty and homelessness. Fortunately, many American families have begun to take in the members of the earlier generations—grandmothers and grandfathers—and thus have recovered for themselves much of their family's precious past. So it must be for the renewed Old First church. It finds itself in the midst of the urban environment where countless grandmothers wander late into the night, carrying shopping bags and sleeping over hot air vents, covered only by thin blankets.

At the other end of the age spectrum, Old First is called upon to salvage and nourish the potential of its youth—babes, children, and adolescents. Becoming a truly multigenerational community will mean gathering alienated youth and abused children and ensuring that infants, still innocent to the incomprehensible vagaries of the world, have some access to a decent life. A disturbingly large and ever-increasing percentage of these American children are members of single-parent families or broken families. The call of Old First churches may be the task of discerning any sociological signals

God may be using in placing so many single-parent families near the doorstep of the church. This is not to glorify the causes of single-parent families or the poverty and ignorance which in all too many instances form the ground from which such families spring. Rather, it is a bold suggestion that the divine call to Christian ministry places less emphasis on the *forms* of human sociality and more on its ultimate purpose. While the form of the single-parent family bears little resemblance to what for many is the ideal, it does represent the will of many persons, primarily young mothers, to lay a foundation for the nurturing of children. Thus if Old First churches are to be faithful to the multi-generational view of the human community, due regard to the welfare of the children, wherever they are found, should be maintained.

The theology for the "new" Old First has profound implications for a Christian understanding of ministry in contemporary society. This theology is one that understands the transcendence of God to be in creative tension with the immanence of God. It is a vision of the God who is *over* all, yet is in so many surprising ways disclosed *through* all that commands obedience in the world. It is a theology which balances redemption of people and places, looking at the whole impact of the Scriptures and attempting to see God incarnate in people. Moreover, it is a theology which does not shirk from attempting to see if there is any "providence in the predicament." Yet living in a predicament is no unfamiliar experience for Old Firsts, proven by a dogged and unrelenting ministry in the wilderness and on the frontier during the formative years of this nation. God's acts in the past still fire the imagination of the descendants of the founders of Old Firsts. Yet the theological vision of Old First, depending as it does on the transcendence of God through all times and places, is one that can support our anguished attempts to make sense of the present and our hope to boldly seize the future.

Chapter 4

Discovering Structures
for Old First Churches

When reading through the case studies of both urban and rural Old Firsts, one generalization stands out: The covenant preceded the buildings and the programs. Notice the founding visions or purposes embedded in some typical Old First cases:

Philadelphia, Pennsylvania. "Nine Christians gathered in a storehouse near the banks of the Delaware River in 1698 to begin worshiping as the First Baptist Church of Philadelphia."[1]

New York, New York. "In 1808 a few African-Americans, armed with their faith in Jesus and strengthened by the mercies already seen, left the worship service of the First Baptist Church of New York City and withdrew forever their membership. These African-Americans, accompanied by a group of Ethiopian merchants, were unwilling to accept racially segregated seating in God's house and determined that they would organize their own Abyssinian Baptist Church—a name inspired by the ancient name of the nation from which the merchants had come."[2]

Boston, Massachusetts. "The history of our church goes back to the year 1665. It was then that nine people, seven men and two women, came together on the 7th of June to form a Baptist organization in Boston."[3]

Columbus, Ohio. "Slavery was a hot issue in the [third decade] of the nineteenth century. Thus, the members of African-American descent petitioned the church (First Baptist), to be set aside as a mission church in 1834. Finally, consent was given in 1836, granting permission for the sisters and brethren to form their church with a special mission."[4]

Wichita, Kansas. "The church was organized on May 26, 1872, with twenty-six members. It was the third church organized in the city and while early records were destroyed by fire it is apparent that there was simply a need for a Baptist congregation that would be a center for evangelism on the frontier."[5]

Paterson, New Jersey. "As believers were added unto the Lord, steps were immediately taken to form a Baptist church, and a council for that purpose was called to meet January 1, 1824.... It took from January 1, 1824, until 1859 for this small congregation to become large enough to erect a large and stately edifice seating 809 people in the heart of downtown Paterson."[6]

Poughkeepsie, New York. "About 1800, George Parker and William Goss and some others began meeting occasionally in each other's homes for worship and Bible study. In July of 1807, about a dozen gathered together in the Parkers' house and decided to form a Baptist Society. [In] 1808 a chapel was built."[7]

Parkersburg, West Virginia. "Under the leadership of Rev. James McAbey, twenty-four people formed the Church of Christ called Parkersburg (Baptist) on October 17, 1817. Fifteen of this group, including Rev. McAbey, had belonged for two years to the Mount Zion Baptist Church near Mineral Wells. Apparently the fourteen-mile trip there caused them to prefer a church within their own small community. Of this group of twenty-four, seventeen were white and seven were colored. According to the covenant into which they entered at either the first or second meeting (in November), they were desirous of enjoying the privileges that appertained to memberships."[8]

Bethel, Ohio. "Our forefathers decided in 1804 to form a new church in order to serve open communion.... From 1822 until 1841 church was held in different homes in the territory until the present building was dedicated on January 1, 1842."[9]

Mount Vernon, Ohio. "A Baptist witness was desired in the county seat so seven people met to form the church [in 1835]."[10]

Several observations strike us immediately. In every case, with or without a pastor, congregations of people came together in covenantal fashion to form the church. Notice also the interesting and different kinds of reasons given for forming a church in each unique context. Notice further that the founding covenants usually included a *spiritual* (worship or evangelism), *geographic* (a town or county seat), *ecclesiastical* (a certain kind of communion or society), and *social* (the "privileges of membership" or admonitions to abide by certain rules of ethics or behavior such as the rule that "you could not hold slaves") commitment.

Again, one cannot help but notice that in the stories of their founding, these and other Old Firsts almost never mention a building as part of the vision of their identity. Indeed, some, like ancient Israel, wandered all over their regions long before they erected their buildings. The original Old Firsts understood that identity was tied to the presence of people and not to the presence of place or building.

As important as organizational structure is in the overall ministry of God's people, the profile of the original Old First does not show great emphasis on this area. This is not to say that Old Firsts were impervious to the importance of organizing people in order to fulfill a mission. Rather, it is an acknowledgment of the fact that Old Firsts put high priority on the covenanting presence of people more than any particular forms of structure or building that covenanting might assume. Whenever organization or structured action did occur it was as simplified as possible, as if Old Firsts never wanted the structure of the action to get in the way of the primacy of the action itself. In terms of architectural history, Old Firsts did not want the form to get in the way of the function; the form needed to follow the function. Thus if one looks at the early history of Old Firsts one discovers that the organizational structure was as simple and straightforward as the simple unadorned edifice in which the people worshiped. For economic reasons the "staff" of early Old Firsts consisted solely of the pastor. Within the congregation itself there was the recognized importance of the role of deacons, whose primary concern was assisting the pastor in the spiritual welfare of members. The congregation also recognized the importance of more mundane matters within the life of faith—matters such as rooftops which needed repairing and pews that needed reseating—and hence the importance of a group of trustees. In addition to these boards there evolved a differentiation of activities within the congregation along gender lines: active women's groups and men's fellowship groups. However, the evolution of these groups must be seen in the context of the patterns of social interaction of the day. With the opening up of the heartland of America in the early nineteenth century and the early West, it was customary for men and women to segregate themselves into bonding patterns that could meet their particular needs.

Essentially then, the structure of the outreach and mission of Old First churches was a simplified one in which the pastor, deacons, and trustees were the primary participants with recognizable lay groups organized along gender lines playing a strongly supportive role. The point here is that the sheer simplicity of structure of the outreach of these churches was but an indication of the primacy of function over form. Faced with the urgency of planting the faith in the context of an oftentimes inhospitable frontier or new and strange surroundings, Old Firsts seized upon the celebratory and missional aspects of the covenant as the primary ways of being the people of God. The celebratory aspects of the covenant required a dedicated preacher. The missional aspects required people who met the perceived needs of other people. Old Firsts knew that a complicated structure was not necessary to accomplish these things.

Many would say the relative unimportance of structure for the historic Old First referred to a time that has long passed—an ideal that is outmoded or naive. To be sure, we do speak of the Old Firsts of a time gone by. We also realize that a simplified church structure may not be a panacea for solving all of the issues that the contemporary Old Firsts face. We are, however, struck by the increasing number of Old Firsts that espouse a simplified organizational structure in the pursuit of their mission goals.

Obviously, a renewal strategy for these churches lies implicitly in the covenantal stories of some of the churches we have cited. Our review of the case studies of the Old Firsts that participated in this study reveals a distinct pattern of churches that are experiencing a sense of renewal and at the same time are espousing a single-board system. Within the last five years First Baptist Church of Watertown, New York, has reorganized itself into a one-board system called a "diaconate." This board is "a strong board and speaks for the church between annual meetings."[11] The Hamilton Square Baptist Church of Trenton, New Jersey, adopted a one-board model after a period of two years of study on the matter. The church made this decision in 1970 and adopted the executive board system, the members of which are a head chairperson and the chairpersons of eight committees, reflecting the total work and mission of the church from worship to administration to community ministry. While First Baptist of Boston did not completely adopt a single-board system, it did streamline its organization and, incidentally, lowered the proportion of the budget devoted to staff salaries to 35 percent. Another good example is the Whitesboro Baptist Church of Whitesboro, New York. In 1983, "after considerable education of the congregation"[12] it adopted the one-board concept. Under this

system an eighteen-member board of deacons was installed and organized into commissions that were concerned with the following:
worship, membership, education, missions, support, and property
management. The members of Whitesboro acknowledge that "the
transition from one form of structure to another has been challenging, but as members become at ease with the concept, they are
discovering ways to operate more efficiently and productively."[13]
First Baptist Church of Oneonta, New York, has adopted a one-board
system; the functions of former boards of deacons and trustees are
now assumed by membership and stewardship committees. At the
Calvary Baptist Church of Washington, D.C., an unsuccessful
attempt was made several years ago to move the church toward a
single board style of organization. At present, however, "many [of
our] leaders hope that we can open that matter for reconsideration
before very long."[14]

Even in cases in which the churches in our study have not moved
to a one-board system, there are attempts to simplify the organizational structure of congregations by recognizing the authority of
organs that have some centralized control or guidance potential.
Many churches now value advisory boards that represent the interests of the constituents in the multiboard system and can articulate
and act on the total vision of the congregation. Such an organ has
immense pragmatic value, enabling the congregation to respond to
emergencies, issues, and concerns with relatively short notice when
the deliberation of the entire church body would not be possible.
First Baptist Church of Philadelphia conducts its ministry within the
context of the coordinating leadership provided by a church council.
This council brings together the presidents of the major boards and
committees for consultation on emergencies and regular meetings
on routine matters of church life. Some may become concerned
that these advisory or church councils might supplant the authority
of the congregation in which every believer has a voice. It is clear
that such organs, while they may act on behalf of the congregation

in the interim between regular meetings of the entire church, are accountable to the entire church for actions taken. The will of the congregation ultimately prevails.

These examples of renewal contain implicit warnings to Old Firsts that have locked onto the idea that their buildings, constitutional structures, patterns of worship, or other programs are fixed and cannot be changed. In many of these churches the sanctuary is the "sanctum sanctorum" and we can easily understand why some congregations esteem their sanctuaries. After all, these sanctuaries represent the labors of their elders, the previous generations that spent their labors and their resources in building a sanctuary for future generations to use and enjoy. God's great acts of the past are remembered there every week when the people recreate the drama of their salvation in worship. Those memories are sacred. The more some Christians experience change and old things passing away, the more some Christians tend to cling to a church that refuses to change. The church may become an anchor but may lose the potential to buoy the congregation up to openness to the future.

Yet, despite the understandable attention congregations may pay to buildings and sanctuaries, the inordinate identification of program with building may lead to a skewed notion of the church's mission, especially in its local setting. The contemporary history of the urban church, for example, is replete with attempts of local congregations to meet the perceived needs of communities by building more buildings or facilities. How often have urban congregations felt that the solution to the problem of youth delinquency or boredom was to build a gymnasium? Burning the mortgage for an expanded wing of the Christian education building has been viewed by many as another indication of increased vigor in programming. Now, one or two generations later, these same churches must hire staffs (who may not be members of the congregation) to run programs in those buildings. Another equally tragic scenario is the report from some churches that they must now rent out the unused space to local groups in order to pay for the cost of heating or cooling these facilities. The visionary mission mode has become a maintenance mode for many congregations.

There is a positive way to view this situation, however. One can say "better a maintenance mode than extinction!" Renting space to pay for heating costs can be seen in a more favorable light if the renters have a constructive impact on the community. First Baptist Church of Philadelphia rents space to Alcoholics Anonymous and the American Association of Retired Persons, serving the double purpose of benefiting the community and maintaining the church.

In the chapter on history, foundations were suggested for the recovery of the mission for Old First churches. History tends to relativize the contemporary fixation on structures because historical reflection shows that the covenant visions preceded the buildings. While many congregations fret over their budgets, schedules, and buildings, they could better use that time seeking to explore their founding vision in a present context.

The covenant of a church reveals the purposes of that church. Coming to terms with this covenant will sensitize people to the current challenges and demands that matter. No one should amputate a building, build a building, or alter a structure without doing some radical reflection on the covenant history of the congregation. However, once the covenantal study has been made, alteration of the building or other structures and programs will probably be required in order to be faithful to the covenant. The relationship between structure and covenant is a central theme that runs throughout this book and is certainly at the core of this chapter.

Old First churches are visually at the center of old communities in an aging nation, where the fastest growing segment of the population is retired or simply old. While some younger churches are talking about their ministry *to* the aging, Old Firsts themselves often embody the ministry *of* the aging. Old buildings, like old bodies, consume energies at levels that leave less resources for bold new kingdom ventures. Everyone recognizes that. One cannot expect dazzling strategies from such churches. Neither can one expect sharply delineated job descriptions outlining who will do *what* for *whom* at precisely what time. The mission thrust of such Old Firsts will not resemble the polished organizational charts of large suburban churches with bright, young business executives on every board and committee. Efficiency, we insist, is not the primary issue for effectiveness in ministry.

Regrettably, we must still be aware that our nation and its "boomer" generation are dominated by narcissism. The unabashed aims of this "Me Generation" have been celebrated throughout the 70s and 80s and that heritage lives with us. "Yuppies," (young, urban professionals) have done their best to celebrate all that is stylish, chic, and self-aggrandizing. In such a culture both old people and neighborhoods are thrown away like paper plates or worn-out jogging shoes. This is the era when municipal bond issues supporting public education or care for those who cannot support themselves usually fail in elections. More to our concern, this is the era when some judicatories and churches in association feel absolutely no responsibility for "Old Mother" churches. In many cases they would just as soon close her down, sell the place, and divide up the profits for the young and strong. Perhaps this image is too strong, but in some denominations it looks like the vultures are circling over Old Firsts.

A Model Celebration

We conclude this chapter with an illustration that shows the wisdom of shaping structure with sensitivity to covenantal history. Once a daughter church decided to celebrate its eighty-fifth anniversary and invited its Old Mother church to a birthday banquet. The entire congregation of the Old Mother church, not very large and mostly older people, was invited to a banquet in their honor. It was the daughter church's way of saying "thank you" to the founding group from the Old Mother church who had started the daughter church in another section of the city in 1891.

During its days of glory, the Old Mother church had started or helped to start more than a dozen churches in that region. The daughter church pictured in this model celebration had in turn started a daughter church that ministered in Spanish, a church which is now flourishing and has grown to approximately the size of the Old Mother church in its heyday.

The party celebrated one hundred years of church growth in that city. Moreover, it created a sense of connectedness in the family of God that had long been lost in that Old First and had never been realized by the third generation of church planting. Most of the Old Mother church members admitted that they did not know that they had started a church in 1891. They had a strong extended kingdom family, but they had not been affirmed for it or invited to a party for many years. Curiously, that situation resembles many contemporary settings. There are old congregations all around us, struggling to stay alive and pay the bills on nearly fixed incomes, and few of us seem to care. By focusing on its heritage in the midst of the mirth of a birthday party, the daughter church rediscovered some of its covenantal history. For the Old First church, celebrating such a history required no elaborate organizational structure or the tedious mounting of multiphased campaigns. What was required was only the will to recover its roots, reach into its history, and reach out to the kingdom family.

That local Old First was able to do this by utilizing a simple organizational model instead of the corporate hierarchical model of many church organizations. It is amazing how many old churches are organized like the companies in the environments around them, with governing boards of directors, work-flow charts, productivity goals, and expectations of hard-nosed staff members. What a radical and ultimately more enlightening idea it would be to organize around theological functions of the church! The´examples cited earlier in this chapter of churches that have moved to simpler structures are ample testimony to a wisdom which happily is making its way into the lives of contemporary Old Firsts. Others seeking renewal should hear this testimony.

Many Old First churches are not finding it necessary to change time-honored structures, constitutions, or boards in order to change directions. Abyssinian Baptist Church in Harlem seems to have used the continuity of the structure to allow significant diversification of affiliations and program during the post-1972 ministries of Samuel Proctor and, now, Calvin Butts. First Baptist Church of Philadelphia has seen a new burst of congregational energy and programmatic diversity under recent-day ministers William Thompson, Peter Wool, and current pastor Dwight Lundgren, but docs not hint at basic structural changes.

In his book *Modern Organizations,* Amitai Etzioni, a contemporary sociologist and student of the theory of organizational behavior, suggests that in the turbulent environments of recent decades where major changes come so quickly, every organization needs some program unit or piece of structure that functions like a research and development component.[15] We propose that Old Firsts take very seriously this idea, working it into the fabric of the church budget. Programmatically, such an idea would mean that somewhere in the congregation someone would be encouraged to dream, take risks, and try some new things. In the past, Old Firsts had within their memberships persons of power, wealth, and status who had executive skills and had managed businesses in crisis environments as part of their everyday work. Today's Old Firsts may not always have those kinds of skills available in their memberships. We propose that denominational executives consider creating management teams of competent and compassionate laity who can serve as support teams for some Old Firsts in the context of genuine caring and renewal.

New Local and Global Roles

Many Old Firsts located in changed downtowns find themselves becoming regional churches by virtue of the changed demographics of their memberships. More and more members have simply begun living in areas farther from the church. This seems to be true across racial and denominational lines. People will travel fifty miles or commute from Milwaukee to Chicago to attend their Old First church. Every Sunday morning some members of Abyssinian Baptist Church will return to Harlem from Westchester or Nassau counties, some thirty or forty miles away. That is powerful loyalty! This is not a new phenomenon, but it does have some new implications concerning the internal dynamics of congregations. While the church expands its base to a more regional scope, the local neighborhoods around the actual church building are undergoing demographic changes in which the ethnic and national background of newcomers is different from the current residents. The chasm between the needs and expectations of the historic commuter members and the new community residents who may be of other racial or language groups presents remarkable new challenges to the structures and programs of Old Firsts.

Changing structures may not be the way to respond to radical change. It may be much more prudent to do the studies of community, history, and congregation and make sure the identity issues are secured and visible first and then begin to branch out in programmatic directions. It is important to make the structural changes after the need for them is clearly demonstrated, rather than make them part of the requirement for change.

Vatican II is proof that when one makes a conscious change in theological focus all sorts of structural changes can and probably will occur in due course. This same reality can be demonstrated in Old Firsts. A new spirit of prayer, care, and will to strike out on bold mission ventures can be the new theological emphasis that makes the structural changes happen. Structural changes at the outset are seldom a priority and in none of the Old First cases did anyone suggest that changes in structure initiated renewal. Rather, they seemed to be the consequences of other initiatives.

The next chapter moves into the discussion of programs for renewed Old Firsts. Even a cursory reading of the cases shows that some "old bones" are springing up with new life.

Chapter 5
The Uniqueness of Ministry in Old First

As we begin this chapter it may be helpful to clarify some terms. "Mission," simply put, is everything the church is sent by God to *be* and *do* in the world. This definition assumes that God initiated the mission of the church and continues to direct it. Likewise, this definition affirms that churches are *sent,* since the very word "mission" implies being dispatched or sent to perform a task or service. As Jesus was sent by God, so Jesus sent the disciples and followers who formed the church. As living embodiments of the living work of Christ, churches are to continue what Jesus began. The church, therefore, is by nature a sign and an agent of the kingdom of God here and now. Everything God rules is kingdom property. That includes everything the church is and does. The church's call to the city to repent and its programs and relationships with individuals and institutions are part of that kingdom mission.

Mission involves everything the church does in response to God's creative and redemptive mandates. Evangelism and mission are not synonymous. Social action is not the same as mission. Discipleship, stewardship, and fellowship, like evangelism and social responsibility, deal with specific and concrete actions. Together these functions become the mission of the church.

Programs are the specific or strategic actions the churches take to implement mission functions. The reality is that while the functions of all churches are the same in every time and place, the forms they take can and indeed must change to fit each unique context. Thus every church will engage in worship. In order to fulfill its functions as a biblically faithful church, a church's worship must be a response to God to whom the church belongs. However, exactly how the church worships (i.e., the kinds of ritually special things it does to show that it belongs to God) will vary from church to church and will depend on many variables. Congregations, like families, have different styles at mealtimes—some formal and some very informal depending upon customs and desires.

Ministry is that loving service of all believers done for God in the church and in the world. Nowhere in the New Testament is ministry the work of a few believers. Rather, it is the expected response of all believing Christians. In a sense then, all church members are ministers for all are called upon to serve. How alien this thinking is to most people! Yet it is critically important for this discussion that we grasp this assertion. Ministry is what the church does, not what a few paid pastors or staff members do, although we have become very comfortable with setting a few people apart to do the work that all are called to do.

The Holy Spirit gives grace to all members of Christ's body. The programmatic task of the church is to inventory those gifts, affirm them, and call them into ministry. This is obviously a very different understanding of church programs than that of many people in America. The rapidly growing charismatic movement is making great strides precisely because its adherents understand that the members are the ministers. Charismatics seek to mobilize everyone—men, women, and children—for ministry. This rediscovery of the gifts and graces of ministers is now creating a renaissance of ministry in Old Firsts as well. The case studies reveal this development.

Before getting into the program specifics, more needs to be said about the historical and theological perspective on ministry of Old Firsts.

Old Firsts have stressed the transcendence of God as Lord of all—including the structures of society. This has implications for mission in that it suggests that God's mission program is not confined to the church or its specific agendas. The Reformation emphasis of Luther and also that of Calvin suggested that one could serve God's mission in a secular calling as a public official or a merchant, artist, or academic.[1] Calvin even suggested that one's vocation itself could serve as a context for worship or indeed a truly sacrificial life. Luther would suggest that a person could serve God by working in a bank, and Calvin would add that any profits would accrue to the glory of God!

Some of the implications for the historic programs of Old Firsts may now be obvious. They have always affirmed the public roles and service relationships of their members in society, and they have seen those member involvements as legitimate programs of the church. Because God was Lord of the city, county, and country, the so-called secular service of the believers was divine service. Programs at the church building, except for worship and education, tended to supplement and support the daily ministries of members who served God by their evangelism and social responsibilities in the world. This is a healthy biblical world view and the rather unique emphasis of ministry in Old Firsts.

Historically then, a large sanctuary in which to hold the worship service might suffice for a church building. Most other ministries could be pursued in the individual members' respective vocational contexts. A new phase in church programs came with the Sunday school and educational programs to build up members for ministries in the world. The "institutional church" with its large staffs and around-the-clock programming came with the influence of urbanization during the latter part of the nineteenth century and the early part of the twentieth century. Such churches were found in the large Northeastern cities, led by people such as Russell Conwell in Philadelphia. At that point Old Firsts took on the semblance of corporate structures in order to meet the social needs of the poor immigrants crowding into America's cities. At that point staff persons became common and the professional ministry categories as we know them today emerged.[2]

We can observe that many Old First churches keep going financially because they rent their facilities to many public or private program agencies. In some instances, this may represent a continuity in mission. Agencies such as the Rotary Club or Boy Scouts are sometimes seen as extensions of the church in the world. In more instances than not, however, a disturbing shift has occurred. On the one hand the church has withdrawn from the world into a self-enclosed structure of religious activities for members. On the other hand the building is brokered to groups who need space. Exceptions to this observation doubtless abound, but for many Old Firsts this represents a tragic schism that keeps activities going. They continue but without a theological commitment or engagement in ministry.

Earlier we observed that this ministry of members in secular environs should be a legitimate program of the church. Now we must add the flip side. Simply holding secular or religious programs in a church building does not necessarily make it a legitimate mission of the congregation. It may be just another manifestation of the chasm created by the congregation's dichotomy between the church and the world.

Two Models of Black Urban Old Firsts

Black churches today may come closest to the historic Old First programmatic ideals. We will examine two programs: Abyssinian Baptist Church in New York City, and Second Baptist Church in Columbus, Ohio.

The modern era of Abyssinian began properly in 1908 when Adam Clayton Powell, Sr., a young gospel giant, became the pastor of the church which had been founded exactly a century earlier in midtown New York City. One hundred years later the people of Abyssinian were a part of the migratory wave of black people who began settling in a promised land of sorts, the treelined and spacious avenues of a place called Harlem. Throughout the twentieth century the identity of Abyssinian's pastors and its people has been inextricably linked to the destiny of Harlem, which was perhaps the most visible symbol of the perils and promise of urban black America. Until Powell's retirement in 1937, a loyal and tithing membership, which had grown to seven thousand, paid the salaries of over two dozen full- and part-time church workers. In addition, they handled the operating expenses of the church and community center and supported a missionary in Africa. The church's motto under Powell was apt: "Forward in a larger service."

Upon the retirement of Powell, his only son, Adam Clayton Powell, Jr., became senior pastor of the congregation. The younger Powell had already begun his service to the church in 1930 as an assistant pastor. He also directed Abyssinian's kitchen and relief operations that fed and clothed thousands of Harlem's needy during the Depression. This intense urge to focus social action through the power of the gospel fueled Powell, Jr.'s election as a city councilman in 1941 and fourteen terms as a Congressman from Harlem beginning in 1944. While wielding enormous power in the nation's Congress, he continued to serve as pastor to Abyssinian's people, exhorting them to be a "light" and "salt of the earth."

Upon the death of Adam Clayton Powell, Jr. in 1972, senior pastor, Dr. Samuel D. Proctor, was called to carry on the tradition of bold and caring leadership of God's people for service in the city. As Abyssinian's senior minister, Dr. Proctor built on the legacy of both Powells. He not only preached the Word of God "in season and out" (2 TIMOTHY 4:2), but also maintained Abyssinian as an uncompromising force and voice for justice, promoting Christian values in community, city, state, national, and international affairs. In recent years, Dr. Calvin Butts has continued a strong ministry following in the traditions for which Abyssian has always been noted.

Abyssinian Baptist Church provides both its congretation and its community with countless resources. A sampling of them include:[3]

ABC FEDERAL CREDIT UNION

A savings and loan agency of the church with officers available to assist members of both the church and community.

ABC FOOD BUYING CLUB

A cooperative venture of both the church and community that purchases food at low wholesale prices and sells to members of the club nutritious food at below retail prices.

ABC CRUSADERS ATHLETIC ORGANIZATION

An athletic program for youth operated through the church under the supervision of a professional athletic director and coaches.

ADAM CLAYTON POWELL, JR. MEMORIAL ROOM

Exhibits of the church may be seen on Sundays and during the week:

Permanent Exhibit. "The Life and Work of Adam Clayton Powell, Jr." recounted through letters, documents, artifacts, photographs, clippings, and volumes.

Special Events Exhibitions. Church history exhibits displaying records from the archives of Abyssinian are mounted during the course of the year in connection with special events.

COUNSELING

Christian and personal growth counseling service for individuals, couples and families provided by the ministerial staff. A social worker is on call. Referrals to outside psychological and psychiatric counseling services are also available.

EMERGENCY FOOD BANK

A service of the church through which non-perishable food is made available to families upon request and on a basis of demonstrated need.

ILAKIKO

A "Big Sister/Little Sister" organization for young women and adolescents.

MUSIC PROGRAM

Sanctuary Choir. An eighty-five member group composed of volunteer singers of various ages, who provide music for the Sunday morning worship services. Each voice section is led by a professionally trained singer. The choir has sung with the New York Philharmonic under the direction of Zubin Mehta in performances that have included excerpts from Verdi's *Requiem* and Handel's *Messiah.* The choir has also appeared in a number of concerts in several other states, at various New York City churches and at the Metropolitan Museum of Art. Primarily, the choir sings anthems, spirituals, oratorios and gospel.

Other choral groups: The Chancel Choir (which performs traditional and contemporary gospel music, spirituals and anthems), the Men's Chorus (which sings spirituals, anthems and gospel), and the Junior Church Choir (which performs a variety of traditional and contemporary sacred music for young voices) appear regularly in worship services of the church on designated Sundays during the church year.

RELEASE TIME

Mid-week non-denominational Protestant religious training for elementary children provided in cooperation with the Board of Education of the City of New York.

SCHOLARSHIPS

Through the Scholarship Committee, the church provides partial scholarships for undergraduates attending accredited colleges and universities in the United States. Special scholarships are available for students who will study pre-med, mathematics, physics, engineering or life sciences.

SCOUTING

Christian scout masters and leaders volunteer with assistants to conduct an ongoing scouting program with Brownies, Girl Scout, Cub Scout, and Boy Scout troops.

TUTORIAL PROGRAM

Tutorial assistance in reading, writing, and mathematics for both elementary and high school children is available on the basis of need during the week.

CLUBS AND AUXILIARIES

Adam Clayton Powell Crusaders
Adam Clayton Powell Memorial Auxiliary
Adam Clayton Powell Overseas Club
Board of Christian Education
Board of Christian Social Concern
Courtesy Guild
Entertainment Committee
Floral Circle
Friday Night Ushers
Junior Usher Board
Mattie Fletcher Powell Volunteer Club
Missionary Society
Nurses Unit
Parent Teachers Association
Pastor's Aid Club
Progressive Ladies' Usher Board
Progressive Men's Usher Board
Satellite Alumnae Club
Senior Ladies' Usher Board
Senior Men's Usher Board
Tiny Tots Choir
Utility Club
Young Adult Ushers
Young Sixties
Youth Council
Willing Workers

SECOND BAPTIST CHURCH OF COLUMBUS

In our second model, Pastor Leon Troy summarizes the ministry philosophy of Second Baptist Church of Columbus, Ohio, in these words:

> I see the church as the central focal point in the inner city. The church has become the gathering place where Christians are equipped through the Word and other instructional training. They must go forth as trained soldiers sharing in the process of the redemption of the world. Therefore, all our resources, time—everything should be directed and given full accountability to God as his agents in this redemptive process.[4]

Some of the ways Pastor Troy and his ministers implement this vision include:

LABORATORY SCHOOL

Serving children ages three to six, the curriculum is based on individualized instruction. While the entire Columbus community was used as a resource and the school enjoyed a large measure of success, inadequate funding caused the program to be phased out temporarily.

POLITICAL FORUMS

Sponsored each year to educate members on local political issues and the views of candidates.

ARTISTIC AND CULTURAL EVENTS

Sponsored by the Black Awareness Education Committee, primarily during Black History Month (February).

SCHOLARSHIP COMMITTEE

Organizes fundraising events on behalf of worthy students and adults who continue their education.

PRAYER COTTAGE

A mobile prayer unit that is taken into the homes of shut-in members unable to come to the regular Wednesday prayer services at noon and 7:00 P.M., meets each week in different homes.

HOME MISSION COMMITTEE

Follows up on various mission projects suggested by members of the congregation and occasionally arranges for speakers from the denominational mission field.

FOOD AND CLOTHING PANTRY

Serves as a repository for people who need emergency assistance. Maintained by the Georgia Miller Circle of the congregation, the pantry is noted for its regular and reliable assistance to persons on public welfare and families in a local public housing unit.

EMERGENCY ASSISTANCE

Persons are referred by the pastor and office staff to appropriate agencies with the capacity to meet needs beyond the resources of the congregation.

BUS MINISTRY

Makes transportation available for the elderly, enabling them to carry on such routine personal affairs as meeting medical appointments or picking up prescriptions. Moreover, the bus ministry enables nearby students at Ohio State University and Franklin University and others without transportation to attend regular worship services.

Other Old First Models

FIRST BAPTIST CHURCH OF WICHITA

While acknowledging that First Baptist Church of Wichita, Kansas, is centering its life more and more in worship rooted in a relational style of ministry (JOHN 13:35), combining love of the believers with the "least of these" (the poor of MATTHEW 25:40 and ISAIAH 58), pastor Roger Fredrikson outlines several program components:[5]

THE TRADING POST

A clothing room and food pantry which serves the poor, transient and the church's own members.

MINISTRY WITH INTERNATIONALS

Primarily serves Southeast Asians (mainly Laotians).

MOM'S DAY OUT

Reaches mothers of young children, including church members and individuals from the community. Children are cared for and taught, providing mothers with free time.

NEIGHBORHOOD CALLING

Members visit those who live within a four-block radius of the church periodically.

THE JAMES GANG

A support group for alcoholics.

PASTORAL ASSOCIATES

A Christian counseling ministry for individuals and couples.

LEADERSHIP CONFERENCE

During the last weekend of August, the Christian Education ministry of the church brings in outstanding leaders to speak and teach to lay leaders from the church congregation and the Wichita Christian community.

RENEWAL CONFERENCE

A three-day conference during the week following Easter with plenary speakers and workshops on renewal.

INNER CITY MINISTRY CONFERENCE

Outside speakers educate the congregation on issues related to ministry in the inner city.

TUESDAY BIBLE STUDY

A lunch-time Bible study ministry to individuals who work in the community.

FIRST BAPTIST CHURCH OF MINNEAPOLIS

Sometimes the contemporary programming of Old Firsts represents a creative departure from traditional programs, as First Baptist Church of Minneapolis, Minnesota, has realized. After enjoying a reputation for many decades as a "leadership church" with a great world vision and an influential pulpit, First Baptist has recommitted itself within the last three years to become "barrier free," both in buildings and in its programs. While it works closely with the city on massive redevelopment plans for the area, twenty-one other identifiable ministries express the vision, compassion, and renewal that has come to yet another Old First:[6]

GUILD

More than one hundred men and women gather each week to make clothes and prepare gift items for mission projects around the world. Over one thousand parcels a year are sent out. This meets weekly and is mainly composed of retired people who have a fellowship meal and devotional period together.

INTERNATIONALS

Once a quarter there is a banquet for international students. Once a month the church provides a meal after the Sunday services and takes the students on a tour of the city to points of interest. Language assistance and visa problems are also dealt with, together with providing them homes and/or accommodations.

DAY-CARE CENTER

Operated independently of the church. Due to lack of funding it had to cease, but we are looking for another group to provide these essential services.

COUNSELING CENTER

This is operated three times a week for those needing counseling in all the areas of human need.

BRANCH 2

Church members assist this Catholic Charities organization by providing soup once a week for all their clients and helping them in their center.

MINISTRY OF JESUS

An outreach to Hennepin Avenue and is a store-front operation. Deals mainly with those who are chemically dependent and provides a spiritual basis for recovery.

SENIOR CITIZENS

A monthly club that provides social experiences for the elderly. Many day trips and sometimes a two- or three-day trip are provided during the summer months. During the winter there are fun events, concluding with devotions.

KINSHIP VISITOR PROGRAM

The church is entrusted with Christ's ministry, is empowered by the Holy Spirit, and exists for a number of purposes: fellowship, service, love, and growth, to name a few. Ministry is not limited to the ordained clergy but is given to all who call themselves Christians. Such ministry is a witness to the living power and presence of God, to offer healing and hope, and to love people. Many of the older adults in the congregation are lonely and longing for some kind of in-depth relationship with another person. This kind of fellowship is exactly the kind of ministry the body of Christ at First Baptist can provide.

SHARE-A-PRAYER

People are invited to call in their prayer requests which are shared with prayer warriors. This operates twenty-four hours a day.

SMALL GROUPS

Bible studies and share-and-care home groups meeting monthly are an important part of our Body Life experience.

YOUTH PROGRAMS

A full range of activities—roller skating, camping, skiing, and swimming parties are scheduled on a regular basis.

CURRENT ISSUE DISCUSSIONS

Every Wednesday evening, after a meal together, the church discusses current issues such as abortion, homosexuality, war and peace, inviting the community.

EVANGELISM OUTREACH AND VISITATION

This meets every Monday and follows some of the principles of Evangelism Explosion.

DRAMA

A quarterly dinner theater where a meal is provided followed by a drama with a Christian theme.

WOMEN'S LOVE BRUNCH

A quarterly meeting on Saturday mornings in the style of Christian Women's Clubs.

SPORTS

Softball, baseball, and golf tournaments are regularly scheduled according to the seasonal interests.

AUDITORIUM

The large church auditorium seating two thousand is made available to the Christian community for programs, concerts, Bible studies, and evangelism outreach.

MUSIC

A full range of music programs which are widely appreciated. Children are a vital part of this and give a concert twice a year. The senior choir does larger and more important Christian works which attract community attention.

LIBRARY READING PROGRAM

Weekly reading group provides encouragement for a wider range of understanding of problems and opportunities facing the Christian church.

RADIO

A radio program which operates on three stations in a three-state area.

OTHER OLD FIRST EXAMPLES

Other examples from our study on renewal are worthy of mention. First Baptist Church of Paterson, New Jersey, reports that their "free Bibles" sign attracts "quite a few to (our) church." When Vacation Bible School ceased to be effective, the church "substituted a Saturday film series instead."[7] Examples of programmatic vigor that have accompanied renewal at other Old First include:

- Golden Age Clubs, family day camps, and "adoption of families" referred by a city mission agency at First Baptist Church in Erie, Pennsylvania.

- Nursery school, housing units for the elderly, day care, and life career planning at First Baptist Church in Boulder, Colorado.

- The "Back Door" nightclub format ministry for teens at First Baptist Church in Jackson, Michigan.

- Al-Anon and Al-Ateen, "Hi New Neighbor," a Holistic Health Library, the "Coalition Against Nuclear Arms" and the "Nottingham Recreation Center for the Physically Limited" are part of First Baptist Church of Hamilton Square in Trenton, New Jersey.

- Lenten lunches, a subsidized housing development, a daycare center for children of working mothers, and refugee re-settlement efforts are among the successful programs at First Baptist Church in Poughkeepsie, New York.

Even the Old Firsts in the relatively smaller communities are expanding to meet the challenges of caring for people. For instance, Lowville Baptist Church, founded in Lowville, New York, in 1824, has recently added a pastoral care team of trained members to its operations. They also added a food pantry, a radio ministry, a tape ministry, and since 1980, a community disaster response ministry for victims of fire and other emergencies who need food, clothing, and shelter.[8]

Clearly, Old Firsts are learning to focus ministries outside the church on target audiences. It is astounding to read the number of cases that mention the levels of awareness of changed contexts and the new ways that congregations can respond. Many struggle with the issue identified in the case of First Baptist Church of Elmira, New York: "The constant question to be addressed is: Is it good stewardship to stay here and spend so much money just to maintain and operate this church building?"[9] Each church must come to its own conclusion by evaluating its unique situation.

It is delightful to see churches developing new theological depth and creativity in worship and a range of Bible study, prayer, and discipleship groups that energize all sorts of outreach ministries. Clearly the spiritual and the social realms are ones that may mutually energize each other.

Finally, in no particular order, let us list some of the kinds of programs seen in Old Firsts regardless of environments. Interestingly enough, renewed Old Firsts do not make fine lines of distinction among the beneficiaries of such programs. They may be churched or unchurched, long-standing residents or newly arrived; it really does not matter. Here are a few of the ministries of some renewed churches:

Housing ministries (all varieties)
Evangelism (all kinds)
Neighborhood visitation
Student ministries (to and by students)
Hobby programs
Music, media, and drama in numerous categories
University or school extension programs
Latchkey programs after school
Clinics (all sorts, including "Well Baby")
Downtowners clubs
Alzheimers support groups
Libraries
Community disaster relief programs
Telephone ministries
Day-care and nursery school
Bible clubs
Ministries to bars, jails, and hospitals
Public witness programs
Nativity scenes
Justice forums

This is the mission of Old Firsts described not so much in theory as demonstrated by practice. The mandate from the Lord of the church continues: be sent to serve as the Son of God was sent. Renewed Old Firsts wear the mantle of servanthood readily and with a good deal of vigor, as these cases have shown.

Chapter 6
Leadership in
Old First Ministry

John Stott, a contemporary Anglican minister and world-mission statesman, has suggested that the number one ingredient of leadership is "vision," and moreover, vision that begins "a holy discontent for things as they are."[1]

Old Firsts have the distinction of having produced and been the beneficiaries of strong leadership. It is interesting to speculate whether the heritage of strong leadership was a consequence or a causal factor in the development of Old Firsts. It should be remembered that almost without exception these Old Firsts represented an implicit "discontent for things as they are." Recall our chapter on history with the exciting sagas of intrepid bands of believers who found no context in which to exercise their beliefs and struck out on their own to parts unknown in their search for religious freedom. Oftentimes in order to form such a community these people had to leave familiar surroundings and the certainty of genteel society and the way of life they had known for so long. Part of the genius of leadership is the ability to articulate and focus a vision for people so that they begin to believe that no sacrifice is too great in the service of fulfilling that vision. The great leaders of Old Firsts must have had that ability. The First Baptist Church of Washington, Pennsylvania, founded on October 14, 1814, remembers strong pastoral leadership in their "story:"

> Everyone knows something of the leadership of our first pastor, the Reverend Charles Wheeler, friend of Alexander Campbell and classmate of the legendary Adoniram Judson.

He was in a true sense the founding father of our church. His pastorate of twenty-four years, the longest in history, set a precedent for long pastorates that has been observed in more recent years.[2]

The Old First case studies reveal another interesting aspect of the phenomenon of leadership in these churches. Besides the conception of leadership that focuses on the outstanding leader—the minister/pastor in these cases—Old Firsts demonstrate the power of vibrant lay leadership as well. While the cases reveal strong pastoral leaders with vision, courage, and the necessary personal resources; average men and women, on the frontiers or in new communities, in many instances developed the outlines of a ministry even before a formal call was issued to a pastor. This interim period tested the inner resources of the laity and helped prepare the foundation for a strong laity that persists to this day. In the context of the times and challenges facing Old Firsts historically, the development of a strong laity was understandable. Oftentimes the most prominent persons in the new communities—the professionals, public officials, and educators—all gravitated toward the local Old First. In doing so they brought skills and a sense of initiative that could not help but enrich the corporate strength of the church. This phenomenon was especially evident in county seat Old Firsts or in the relatively small towns where the Old First held a commanding position.

For the most part, however, the laity of Old First churches was very similar to that of an Old First in Plainfield, New Jersey. First Baptist Church of Plainfield was organized by a strong group of "mostly farmers" in 1818, including some descendants of believers who had fled from religious persecution in Europe. After organizing the congregation of eleven men and twenty-three women (including one "colored"), they met to adopt their articles of faith and then asked Elder Jacob Fitz Randolph to become their pastor.[3]

The current leadership in these churches has appropriated the essence of the leadership tradition in the Old First mold.

The case studies show an impressive depth of commitment by pastors whose longevity of service sometimes extended to four decades and by members of extraordinary abilities whose minds, hands, and resources left an incredible imprint on Old Firsts. While our findings are obviously somewhat tentative, we nevertheless are persuaded that they point to decidedly verifiable trends within Old Firsts today.

In summary, Old Firsts more often than not had strong visionary, pastoral leaders who were not afraid of taking risks, who inspired people with their great preaching gifts, and who had the ability to be flexible in often inchoate conditions. While in many instances these Old First leaders spent the bulk of their active ministries in small communities or frontier towns, they were not without an appreciation of classical education and were not ashamed to combine intellectual rigor with evangelical efforts.

During the National Consultation on Old First Church Ministry in Pittsburgh, participants were invited to suggest characteristics that they felt would be specifically desired in pastoral leadership for the 1980s and beyond. Their suggestions were grouped under two headings: attitudes and abilities. The attitudes they listed were:

1. A sense of call and commitment to Jesus Christ.
2. A sense of humor and optimism.
3. Flexibility.
4. A strong sense of direction.
5. A biblically oriented vision or perspective on the city and the church.
6. A sense of trust in people.
7. A healthy mix of urgency and patience.
8. An informed perspective on the environment.
9. Mature, realistic love—"tough love."
10. Personal discipline.
11. Personal ego security—the freedom to fail.

12. Imagination and innovation.

13. A willingness to live in community.

14. A sense of history.

15. A strong commitment to the gospel as enacted in the local and global perspectives.

16. Personal stamina.

17. Commitment to marital and familial enhancement—"peace in the parsonage."

Abilities were:

1. To communicate effectively on both a personal and corporate level.

2. To manage and administer operations effectively.

3. To be able to establish "presence" with people.

4. To know when to delegate duties and responsibilities.

5. To understand the power of symbols and their role in worship and in the life of a congregation.

6. To be able to celebrate corporate life joyously.

7. To be able to study and grow.

8. To be able to find resources for support.

9. To be able to accept people as they are.

10. To serve as a model for the gospel and to enable the congregation to live out the gospel.

11. To be able to live creatively with ambiguity and unfinished tasks.

12. To have the ability to set priorities for oneself.

13. To have an attitude toward ecology that sees the wisdom in recycling.

14. To be able to preach with power.

15. To be able to cope with conflict.

16. To be able to think theologically and biblically about the church's life.

17. To understand and live out the servant role of pastor.

18. To be able to function effectively with multilingual and multiethnic groups.

It would be well to remember a few things as we reflect on the attitudes and abilities noted above. First, one should remember that these traits were the ideal attitudes and abilities judged by the participants of the Old First church consultation to be desirable characteristics of pastoral leaders of renewed Old First churches. At the same time the participants were familiar with effective leaders of Old Firsts who had possessed the characteristics they had listed. Therefore, while these were ideal types, they did have a measure of reality about them. As such, they could serve as a measure of the leadership quality of the pastoral leader in any real-life Old First church setting.

Upon reflection, participants in the consultation decided that an implicit characteristic for model leaders was the ability to handle paradox. Throughout this book and indeed throughout the study, the authors were struck by the notion that the present situation of many Old Firsts is a paradoxical one: Once powerful bastions of the culturally mighty and the politically influential, Old Firsts stand in many downtown areas like aging dowagers, who, realizing that the family fortune is depleted, have resigned to derive whatever glory there may be left to the family name. Strong leadership is necessary to help people overcome any possible shame they may feel as they reflect on the fallen status of Old Firsts. The genius of effective leadership in this situation is the ability to *transcend* the paradoxical situation. Vigorous articulation of the vision of what Old Firsts were and what they can become is a part of what strong leadership in this context means.

However, there is another aspect of paradox in the leadership picture of Old Firsts. As you scan the ideal attitudes and abilities, notice that many of these traits appear to be mutually exclusive, at least on the surface. One is called upon to be flexible but also to have a disciplined sense of direction. The leader is expected to embody urgency and patience at the same time. The leader is expected to be so secure in ego strength that fear of failure will not be a problem. The leader should be able to accept people where they are and have the vision to lead them to where they need to go. More-over, the leader is expected to embody "tough love" a mature and realistic display of loving. With such an attitude, it is important to be careful in making a distinction between emotion and love that has as its aim the total welfare of the person loved. Finally, the leader should embody the servant role in the congregation yet be comfortable with power, so much so that responsibilities and duties can be delegated with some degree of authority.

This reflection on the paradoxes inherent in the desired leader-ship profile of Old First is not intended to suggest that fulfilling all of the expectations in the profile is impossible nor that the leader of Old First is doomed to failure for not living up to an ideal. Far from it! We are persuaded that any paradoxes inherent in the leader-ship profile do not point to mutually exclusive traits but actually lead to mutually affirming facets of the notion of being called to service in Christ. A call to this service helps put in better perspective all of the elements of the leadership profile which may appear to be mutu-ally exclusive. One begins to realize that accepting people where they are does not preclude affirming their potential. Thus it is possible to accept people where they are and yet lead them to positions where they have never been. One may also begin to realize that attaining the freedom to fail may not be such an outrageous proposition if one takes the position that no tactic or strategy in the service of Christ's mission is ultimate, and that as far as the Christian is concerned the only ultimate act should be the confession that we belong to Christ and his kingdom. Many effective leaders of Old Firsts struggle with different strategies in attempts to become renewed. They must feel that God will take care of the mistakes as long as we take care to be faithful. Finally, the servant/leader paradox is wholly familiar to Christians who struggle with the problem of power and what to do with it. Christians who are called apart for leadership have a special duty to remember (MATTHEW 23:11, RSV): "He who is greatest among you shall be your servant." For those leaders who secretly struggle to balance clear and unequivocal ego enhancement with the image of servanthood, it should be remembered that the servant is always of value to his or her Lord and to the mission on which he or she is sent. Just as the leader must accept his people, the leader should always be aware of the truth that Christ always accepts and gives full worth to his servants.

In addition to these attitudinal skills and abilities of leadership, pastoral leaders in the Old First context must have a certain intellectual rigor. A couple decades ago John Fry, a Presbyterian minister in the Woodlawn area of Chicago, set the church world on its heels when he led his congregation in granting sanctuary to members of the Blackstone Rangers, one of the more notorious youth gangs of Chicago. Fry went so far as to allow the gang members to store their weapons in the church. Having gained the confidence of gang members, Fry became known as a symbol of the church's intention to develop a viable ministry to youth gangs. This was contextualization of the gospel in its rawest form. For all of his work in exploring the radical imperatives of practical theology, however, John Fry always affirmed a basic intellectual preparedness in his work. He went so far as to say that anyone who could not properly exegete a passage of Scripture in the original language in fifteen minutes was not worth the calling to the ministry. Fry's posture calls to task those in the theological world and the church who believe that practical theology does not have the intellectual rigor of other areas of theological study. Fry would probably argue that because the pastor must always be in a position to articulate and interpret the church's biblical, historical, and theological roots in an effective manner, such a leader is probably called upon to have more intellectual gifts than are normally appreciated. Contextualizing the gospel or contemporizing the message of faith is no easy task. One must be able to *interpret* the essence of the original Christian message to contemporary minds and ears so that the original urgency is not lost. If one does not have a sure handle on the essence and what it meant in its original context, something will surely be lost in the translation. An important aspect of pastoral leadership will be rendered ineffective. Just as speaking two or more languages implies an intellectual mastery of the meaning of symbols in two or more systems, so does the ability to interpret for others the meaning of the gospel in a contemporary setting. The intellectual imperative of pastoral leadership demands that one be an exemplar of multi-cultural, multilingual, and multiracial proficiency. Pastors must be able to speak more than one "language" whether that language is understood in terms of ethnic and cultural patterns or linguistic systems. Biblically, such proficiency has distinct precedents in the figures of Moses, Esther, and Ruth. Moses was able to speak the language of the Pharaoh's court and yet understand the cries from the huts of his people. Esther was able to save her people through her ability to comprehend the circumstances of the Persian court. In the visionary mode of servanthood, the pastoral leader is called upon not only to expound the ideal of multicultural contact, but also to live it out by intellectual mastery of many systems.

The final pages of this chapter will be devoted not so much to a further discussion of leadership, but to the challenges such leadership might make to various groups within the life of the church. As we reflect on the importance of leadership for the future viability of Old Firsts, and indeed for the whole church, we believe that certain segments of our common life in the church ought to be mindful of some things.

First, we urge the local churches to be especially cautious and mindful of the grave importance of choosing a pastoral leader or pastoral leadership team. As we have attempted to show, leadership is probably the most crucial variable in the renewal of Old Firsts. The recovery of history is important, and the focus of theological rationale for program and structure is necessary. But none of this is likely to happen and be sustained if there is no bold and caring leadership. Someone must be able to articulate and make sense of the overall vision in which recovering history and focusing a theological rationale for programs and structure takes place. That crucial "someone" is the pastoral leader.

While choosing the pastoral leader is of utmost importance, choosing the search committee for such leadership is equally important. We realize the importance of making sure that such committees be representative of the entire makeup of the church and that the concerns of various interest groups be heard. However, of equal or even greater importance than one's interest group is the interest potential members of the search committee have in understanding the dynamics of recovery and renewal. These members should show the ability to articulate how leadership relates to these dynamics and how such leadership would enable the church to move toward renewal. This ability is of greater importance than membership in one of the several interest groups of the church.

Local churches are therefore urged to seek and secure the most able leadership possible after a deliberate search process involving conscious assessment of how such leadership would facilitate the dynamics of renewal. Such persons are to be called to leadership, not merely because they are available or fit a prescribed mold, but because they genuinely meet the criteria for the best pastoral leader.

We similarly urge seminaries to set higher standards of commitment and promise for entry of students and recruit accordingly. We are impressed with the old Jesuit model of theological training that immersed prospective members of the order in rigorous scholarly and spiritual disciplines. When and if they made the grade, they were sent out into the toughest of environments. This chapter has already suggested the critical importance of intellectual rigor for the pastoral leader. However, spiritual formation and preparation is equally important for the novice in theological studies. While we do not suggest that there should be a spiritual litmus test for preseminarians, we do, however, wonder if the professional Christian ministry might devise procedures to ensure some suitable *aptitude* for spirituality, if not correct *attitude* toward spirituality. The point is not to create another hoop of orthodoxy through which people have to jump. However, we do consider the aptitude or openness to spirituality to be of legitimate interest to the professional ministerial guild and the church which the guild serves.

Seminaries provide a vital function in training leaders for the church. It is very obvious that centers of learning must exist to provide tools to exegete both the Word and the world, both Scripture and the social contexts of the congregations. We are impressed both with how necessary this is and how few seminaries seem to be doing it.

The authors also have a word of challenge and hope for pastors of Old Firsts. As we examined the case studies, we were overwhelmed by the pluralism and complexity of these contexts and congregations in which pastors serve. We are aware of the great deal of ego strength that is necessary to handle the marginality built into many pastoral situations, especially in troubled churches in troubled environments. In private conversations pastors have shared their periodic feelings of inadequacy and a sense of being overwhelmed with the task of helping to breathe life into what appear to be lifeless bodies. No doubt many pastors overcompensate for their feelings of inadequacy, frustration, or anger by resorting to cynicism or coercive, authoritarian schemes. As a result of cynicism, many pastoral leaders begin to take a combative stance toward the local church and denominational hierarchies. Others, proceeding from a feeling of distrust, devise elaborate organizational structures that can insulate boards from boards, auxiliaries from auxiliaries, and finally people from people. Burnout and/or mutual resentment between pastor and people could result. However, we see reasons for hope.

Robert K. Greenleaf has written a most helpful book, entitled *Servant Leadership: A Journey into the Nature of Legitimate Power and Greatness.* For Greenleaf, servant leaders choose to be a force for good *inside* the institution. They have the ability to listen with sympathy and effectiveness and then withdraw to set their own priorities. They have, he suggests, a feel for patterns, overarching conceptual insights, and the unknowable and unseeable; they know how to look for the "big picture."[4] It is our contention that appreciation for the big picture helps to relativize personal failures and pretensions to corporate grandiosity. Pastors should understand that the relative turbulence in any congregation is not anyone's fault or any one person's responsibility. Conflict may be a necessary component in organizations, even religious organizations. Perhaps it is more necessary in the latter since these organizations' opinions and positions on issues are inevitably linked with perceptions of ultimacy. Thus pastors need to understand that conflict may be a natural outgrowth of simple organizational dynamics and not necessarily an indictment against their interpersonal skills.

Observers of congregational behavior confront a wide variety of leadership styles and congregational configurations. There are many models of church leadership and organization, each appropriate in particular contexts. Obviously, God's spirit is renewing many Old Firsts, and the specific tool kits of the pastors vary a great deal. The case studies have confirmed that assertion.

If a pastor or a leadership team has been in place for at least two decades, they probably have seen several waves of change sweep over their congregation. The post-World War II "baby boom" generation has now raised their families and established values for their lifestyles. Like so many consumers, Americans in the 1990s seek religious experiences and philosophies of life that give meaning to their personal lives. Sometimes these persons want to avoid lasting commitments or institutional loyalties. Religion for many is seen in pragmatic terms as a necessary appendage to a lifestyle that glories in finding the "gusto" in the good life. Enlightened leaders who can reach these persons and who are secure enough to listen to them can help create a climate in the church which is safe for diversity.

Recent conversations with two long-time Chicago pastors of old churches, one black, one white, representing Catholic and Evangelical traditions, revealed that both have multiple worship programs with music and liturgy that is targeted for different audiences. Both pastors expect God's gifts to emerge from the congregation as the Spirit calls and not because of rational program development or strategic long-range planning. Both churches are growing rapidly in troubled inner-city areas, in contrast to many around them. Both attribute such growth to having made "caring in the name of Jesus" a major theme in all that is done. People are nurtured in the name of Jesus. All manner of around-the-clock caring groups and programs emerge from the needs of the people. The leaders stimulate and facilitate, but neither of these pastors try to control or force the programming into existing or traditional patterns and structures. Both view themselves as coaches, not players. Both have helped establish stricter membership requirements, in contrast to the rather loose expectations in many main-line denominations, and both attract more and more people each week. One suspects that the ability of these leaders to embody the richness of the truly committed life has accounted in large part for the renaissance in their churches.

As we look for leaders we look to people like Moses. He was raised in a nontraditional home with at least one resourceful parent, given an excellent education, and introduced to field experiences. We look for someone who could take a group of grumbling brick makers and ghetto dwellers from Egypt into the toughest environment in the Middle East and from there send them on to the Promised Land. But we must be realistic. Moses was a unique leader of whom it was written posthumously, "and there has not arisen a prophet since in Israel like Moses" (DEUTERONOMY 34:10). There are not many men or women with all of his gifts. There never were many. However, God does love Old Firsts and will raise up prophets for them. Just as Moses emerged from an unlikely place, leaders for Old Firsts will emerge from unexpected situations.

Chapter 7
A Word for Others

Although this book has grown out of discussions and concerns expressed within the American Baptist Churches, there are many primary principles and guidelines offered in this book that may be significant for other ministry institutions. This chapter seeks to include these other groups.

Many Old Firsts have become rather small, but the image of Old First presented as the norm for our discussion in this book is the larger institutional church with multiple staffs. We have sought to affirm and renew these smaller institutions as integral to God's kingdom. It has at least been implicitly argued that they have unique roles and resources that were never more needed than at this point in time. We hope you can agree.

We hope you do not assume that a small church is rendered less significant than larger churches. There are many church models that are valid. Each has unique contributions. No one model can exhaust God's agenda in a given region. This chapter addresses the issue of specialization in church models as a way of meeting the challenge of growing social or environmental pluralism.

The following church models can be found in nearly every region of this country. Each church is different. Each can reach people that others cannot. Each has a different leadership tool kit. They are like an ecclesiastical flower garden. Which is best? Who can say? It is like asking which is better, a blender or a wooden spoon? It depends entirely on the task and other resources of the one making the choice!

Here are a number of models:

The cathedral or ecclesia—a highly visible and symbolic center of church authority, a historic regional church.

The denominational mission church—a new church that has been developed as a result of a planned strategy of outreach or growth.

The ethnic church—a church that might not function in the language of its "mother country," but still retains a degree of the cultural ethos of that country.

The house church—a small, informal group based on a New Testament model, involving families and close friends who seek to express their faith relationally.

The immigrant church—a first- or second-generation phenomenon that attempts to transplant the religious ethos of a native land.

The intentional community—a contemporary, often single-generational expression of high commitment and faith functioning both as a sign of the recovery of a particular vision and in psychological response to the hunger of many people for a spiritual alternative.

The international church—a church that may draw persons of diverse national backgrounds who wish to escape the nationalistic constraints of the ethnic church.

The media church—a rather recent phenomenon in which a congregation functions as the "stage props" for large radio, television, or educational ministries.

The multilanguage cluster church—often found in transitional urban neighborhoods, these churches provide a residence for several language groups which meet at different prearranged times.

The new charismatic church—a form of congregational life that stresses a worship style that is highly experiential, encourages speaking in tongues, and offers healing to believers.

The parish neighborhood church—a church that functions in a sense as a chaplain to a neighborhood, very much in the European parish model.

The storefront church—a rather unique urban response to the sense of marginality many persons may feel in mainline denominations and churches. These congregations are led by a strong charismatic figure. They rent space in commercial buildings in their primary stages of development en route to more permanent quarters.

The corporate independent church—a highly organized and denominationally independent congregation with a complex program and structure organized along corporate lines whose expressed aim is to grow and reach as many people as possible.

The established mainline church—churches of this sort belong to the denominations generally understood to be in the Reformed tradition, as well as Anglican traditions like the United Methodist and Episcopal churches. These churches make up the bulk of Protestantism in America.

The historically independent black church—while generally espousing the theological tenets of mainline Protestantism, historically independent black churches owe their origin to the historic revolts against the racism practiced by some of these denominations in the latter eighteenth and early nineteenth centuries.[1]

After reflecting on the history and destiny of Old Firsts, our admonition is for you to be faithful to your theological mission, your unique heritage, and your own changing contexts. Do not imitate. Seek to discover your own call from God and the gifts the Holy Spirit has given you for kingdom witness. We have words for other bodies as well.

To *daughter churches,* this is no time for arrogance just because you have grown larger and have more resources than your parent congregation. In some cases you are now Spanish and your mother church was English, Swedish, or German. In other cases you are now black and your mother church was white. To be sure, mother churches are not always kind, and you may remember the condescension and outright hostility your own mother church showed you. Nevertheless, it is time for you to become reconciled to your mother church and be available should help be needed for her renewal; the sake of God's greater mission in your region may require it. It might be a good idea for you to have a banquet in her honor as you celebrate your next birthday. Thank this Old Mother church for your birth, regardless of however inauspicious or painful the circumstances surrounding that birth may have been. God can be glorified in such a celebration. In certain instances this type of historical reflection has revived the spirits and zeal of the family of God. Some divorces and separations in the family of churches are residual scandals that have muted our clear testimony to the grace and forgiving spirit God wishes to prevail. Take initiative. Be reconciled to God and neighboring congregations so that the whole body of Christ in your region may be whole again and able to minister with a clear conscience.

To *denominations,* we urge you never to forget that you are heirs to the associational urges of early Old First churches. In a very real sense, Old Firsts helped create your associations, synods, conferences, and presbyteries. You have inherited their national, educational, and foreign mission agendas and have benefited the longest from their combined resources. Now the roles have reversed for many Old Firsts. You may be asked to do "mission in reverse" with all the integrity that implies, for "*to whom much is given, will much be required.*" (LUKE 12:48). Consultant teams may direct some of the resources back to the Old Firsts to enable them to renew and address their new opportunities with strength and vigor. Some new models may be necessary for this, but all sorts of creative linkages are possible and can be implemented for the glory of God and the strengthening of our total witness.

To *Old Firsts of other denominations,* we as American Baptists think our Old Firsts have more in common with you than with many other models of church life in our own denomination. For that reason we share our findings with you in this book and invite you to a new forum in ecumenical dialogue. We think our Old Firsts are laboratories for globally significant outreach ministries that can link mission at home and abroad in creative ways.

As we all try to reach increasing numbers of refugees coming to our shores and our cities from turbulent areas of the world, we need to share some common agendas and some common ways we can stand together to work for Jesus. We can also profit from your critique, and we invite you to speak the truth to us in love to help keep us honest and biblically faithful in our stressful times and places.

To *the "church universal,"* this book has attempted to reflect on a bit of American religious history and describe the witness of a group of God's churches in the old New World. While some of these churches are nearing their three-hundredth birthday, they are quite young by the standards of other congregations in the Church Universal found in Europe, Africa, and the Middle East. On the other hand, they are much older than the churches that are springing up in Latin America, Africa, and Asia. This is a part of our history you should know about and profit from. It is time to build a bridge between us. We have some concrete suggestions:

First, we invite your help and ask that we be forgiven for our triumphalism, arrogance, and paternalism in the past. We do not find it easy to admit that we need help from anyone—especially foreign congregations that are mission aid. But we do! Some of our Old Firsts are located in neighborhoods euphemistically called "Third World USA." Structural injustice, racial prejudice, mounting human need, and rising human greed abound in the shadow of our buildings. We can no longer cope, much less grow, in the midst of these new realities. Many of us are tired and do not have the spiritual will or the physical resources to deal with these issues. A new kind of "mission in reverse" is in order here whereby you may send resource persons who can help us serve the international migrant streams in our places of worship. In other cases, please send missionaries to us! Help us learn languages and create the new mission structures we never had to think about in the past.

Help us develop yoked parishes that can express our solidarity in a transnational world that no longer respects conventional borders. We know that international migration and the effects of the dislocations in national economies is our lot now as well as yours. Until now we have largely been spared the agonies and therefore the tragic lessons of such developments.

The fruit of the foreign missionary programs come now to our country in larger numbers, but often they pass us like ships in the night. These people, as new immigrants, acknowledge few of our linguistic needs and little of our cultural heritage while very conscious of their need to preserve their own. We think it is time we create a forum to rethink the historic issues faith and culture so that we can work together with true communion and integrity. We freely acknowledge the extent to which our faith is held captive by our culture. Thus while we want to reach out to you, we unfortunately prefer to do so as long as the music and format of our regular 11 A.M. worship services are not altered. Until your arrival many of us did not realize how much cultural baggage we had accumulated over the years. We need your wisdom and counsel here even as the first church in Jerusalem needed counsel after it became ethnically and linguistically diverse (ACTS 15). To borrow a line from C. S. Lewis, we really were "surprised by joy" to find you next door. We think we should receive you as God's latest gift to our country and communities, but we do not always show it or accept your presence in our midst. Frankly, we feel a bit threatened.

Yet, as we realize, most of the world is now in transition. You will profit from a dialogue and partnership with us as much as we will from a dialogue and partnership with you because your own Third World cities are also filling up with people from many backgrounds different from your own. We can help each other as internationally yoked Old Firsts sharing our histories and resources in our multiple contexts.

To *dead or dying Old Firsts,* we candidly admit that in some neighborhoods Old Firsts cannot be renewed. They must either relocate (in which case they really are no longer Old Firsts and should probably get a new name), or have a grand funeral truly worthy of their past attended by members of the family of God. Sometimes persons using creative "estate planning" leave legacies for ongoing mission. These legacies can accomplish far more than artificial life support systems put in place for lots of good reasons but with little regard for ultimate kingdom realities. Some places need new wineskins. In such places it is terrible to see so much effort wasted by God's people. They work feverishly to rearrange the deck chairs on the Titanic while the crew abandons ship in guilt or goes down in dubious martyrdom. Lest we be accused of too ghoulish a tone here, we are not asking for ecclesiastical undertakers to rush into situations that appear dire on the surface but in reality are not hopeless. We are asking for far-sighted denominational executives to develop globally significant strategies worthy of revitalized Old Firsts. We need caring networks that will share resources and, in that context, create the mechanisms that allow death with dignity only when and if such action is appropriate.

To *historic mission agencies and societies,* we recall fondly how our histories intersected at critical stages in the effort to meet the needs of people in our nation. We were allies in the great reform movements of the nineteenth century; we were allies in the effort to provide basic social services to immigrants and migrants in the urban centers of the last century and even in the present time. In rescue missions, YMCAs, Bible societies, Salvation Army posts, settlement houses, and city mission societies, we have lived and worked together.

Today some of you have been renewed or have found new transformed purposes. Others have abandoned their historic theological commitments altogether, becoming merely another program agency in the United Way drive. However, let us say "thanks" for all you meant to us and take a new look at our areas of service and interest. We will need help to reach beyond the boundaries of even renewed Old Firsts to tackle the effects of so many current issues: latchkey kids and single-parent families, the flight of capital from our communities, bank foreclosures on our farms and key industries, the scandalous increase of drug abuse, alcoholism, and mental illness, to say nothing of the stress of life with toxic wastes in our water, air, and food chain.

Surely Old Firsts and their historic allies can come together on these issues for another campaign. We think some of the same principles and conditions necessary for our renewal can be laid at your doorstep as well, and in gratitude and hope, we do so.

To *denominational colleges and seminaries*, we are aware that demographics do not bode well for your immediate future. We share your concern that through the end of this century the ranks of youths, 18-28, will be declining. We have never needed you more than now. However, with some good reasons we think you may be planning to widen your nets and abandon your longstanding relationship with us in search of more profitable constituencies with available and ready cash.

Frankly, we sympathize with you. However, we suggest that you learn from our study and reflection process about what it means to be a renewed American Baptist institution. While we are not those who believe in bowing to the idols of tradition for their own sake, we issue a word of warning to institutions that may be tempted to scuttle tradition in favor of what is more expedient for the moment. We think that now is a unique time in the history of American higher education for American Baptist colleges and seminaries to renew a larger vision—a vision which recovers much of the vibrancy of the past. We are Baptists in what Martin Marty has called an era of the "Baptistification of the world." We think our free-church tradition is now "cutting edge" ecclesiology on six continents. We would urge therefore that strategic planning be pursued in tandem with a sharpened mission statement of the institution that points to the recovery of your mission in the world of higher education. Marketing and mission may go hand in hand; there need be no dichotomy between planning and faithful purpose.

We can be faithful to the past without being shackled to it. One remembers how Henry Ford doggedly hung on to the Model T far beyond its useful life (or product cycle). He did so because he was so invested in the original product and all of its glory that he refused to reevaluate the creative process. Ford boasted that he could give America any car it really needed, as long as it was a Model T and was black! As a result of his shortsightedness, he literally shut down Detroit at great cost and hardship because he refused to recognize the changing climate of the country and the demand for more varied styles of automobiles.[2]

Finally, we believe that our own National Ministries of the American Baptist Churches USA, needs to set an example in this grand enterprise of the recovery of mission. This unit of the denomination began its work more than 150 years ago with three major mandates: (1) to do evangelism, (2) to plant new churches, and (3) to care for persons in special need.

Over the years many accretions came along and were added; new times demanded new mandates. Unfortunately, the primary vision struggles to survive at all in some cases.

How about a creative return to these basics? We urge a *return, not a reaction* to advice from some quarters to seek a simpler vision in a simpler time of yesteryear. While these historic mandates are simply stated goals, they will demand more than simplistic actions. They will demand that some sophisticated planning be done to bring them into reality. For example, what would a budget look like divided equally among the three categories mentioned above? What kind of new words in the vocabulary of faith would have to be created in order to speak to persons who have been so jaded by a culture of narcissism? Struggling to answer these questions in pursuit of our three goals would usher in a contagious, new energy and radical vision that could serve as a model for a renewal process for all aging institutions. Perhaps those three original purposes need to become four or five or more; perhaps not. Again, faithfulness to the past is not a matter of exactitude but a matter of attitude. In any case, without the reexamination of theological vision and mission purposes, strategic planning for ministry will be impossible for American Baptists or anyone else. The barriers to effective process in the denomination are the same as in the local Old First church: they are internal and political, including questions of self-definition and corporate purpose. The more we think about these realities, the more convinced we are that we need to renew the mission and denominational structures of Old Firsts simultaneously.

As we said in the beginning of this chapter, we have written this book primarily for and about American Baptist Old First churches. However, the more you look at this phenomenon, the more you will learn about yourself.

Turning Around Old First Churches at City Center

Many of our doctoral students and ministry colleagues have used this book to help congregations build a foundational, theoretical and theological basis for change. Many also supplemented their reading with management literature from business "turn-arounds" (a CEO specialization in today's global marketplace). Like corporate CEO's, some pastors of churches are so wedded to their products and programs that they can't muster the emotional strength of executive courage to change them. Their own personal identity and psyche is at stake. They are survivors, and for one or more reasons, they can't dream and lack the energy for big-picture analysis. Such pastors are unable to signal their colleagues that change can or even should occur.

Meanwhile, the major revolution occurring in God's church worldwide is the emergence of the laity as the leaders of ministry in the church and in our communities. Many pastors feel threatened by this course, but wise pastors will enlist lay members and serve as their coaches, consultants and cheerleaders for the renewal process.

The Three Stages of the Renewal Process

THE DISCOVERING PHASE

The simple formula is to take between ten and twenty percent of the congregation and create what we might call the "task force for congregational transformation." While creating this group, some have found that it works best to use a diagonal cut of official and non-official church members from different constituencies and generations within the church. So, the task force may have twenty or more persons, depending on the size of the congregation. Remember a rule of thumb in organizational change: If about 20 percent of an organization adopts change, they will be significantly able to influence the remaining 80 percent most of the time.

Now, divide the task force into four sub-groups, each of which will have a distinct role during the discovering phase. So the diagram looks like this as we add:

- the history team
- the community team
- the congregational team
- the "spy" team

The history team organizes to review the entire history of the church. They read the official documents and they interview the oldest members. They not only read the minutes of business meetings, but they try to read between the lines or even behind the decisions made long ago. Soon it should become clear to the history group that there are recurring themes in the life of this church, themes which re-emerged during different pastorates and in times of special stress (wars, depressions, conflicts, etc.). This group will report their findings at quarterly meetings of the task groups and at periodic meetings of the congregation. Historical reflection is not to indulge in nostalgia or imitate old patterns. History gives permission. Ask "why" the church built here? Why did we do thus and so? Interview older members and you will doubtless uncover some courageous, even radical traditions in the past. It is important for this group to be asking questions like this: "Given the decision they made then, what do we think those pioneers would have done with this or that contemporary issue?"

Meanwhile, the Community Team is investigating the changes underway outside the church buildings. This group will talk to city and community leaders. They will see what the school system and health care system is learning, as well as the police and politicians. Surely in all this, there are niches for this and other churches. The traditional audiences of the community may be moving away, but others are taking their place. More and more this group will be asking, "How would we design our ministry if we are to take this or that population seriously?" Put simply, evangelism is "scratching people where they itch in the name of Jesus."

The Congregational Team is starting with the membership and attendance as it is; not as it used to be. They are spending time with them asking questions like: "How did you come to know Jesus?" and "How did you find your way to this church?" "What drew you and kept you here over the years?" Most denominations have materials for assessing the spiritual giftedness of your members. Sadly, however, many older churches organize members into roles and functions motivated often by loyalty and guilt rather than giftedness. That wears thin after a while. Members carry expectations and visions. Seek to uncover those and nurture them. While you can't do everything, begin to describe and communicate the strengths and capacities you do find among your people as opposed to the limits and deficiencies they may seem to possess. In subsequent stages, you can begin to build on those "islands of strength," the surprising capacities you have uncovered.

The "spy" team will organize itself to visit and call other churches both near and far, both within and without your denomination. What are other city center churches, or congregations in our kind of situations learning and doing? Some incredible new programs have emerged around the USA, in Europe and beyond in city center congregations. We need not reinvent every wheel here. The kingdom is bigger than our church, and the good news is that many wonderful things can be learned and shared. Hope is a powerful motivator. Frankly, we think it is a good idea to call up every bishop or denominational leader and ask questions like: "If you had to prove that God were alive in city center, what would you point to?" Our experience is that Catholics, Orthodox, Protestants, Evangelicals and Charismatics alike love to share their stories and they can learn much from each other.

It may not take an entire year for this discovering process, but in some ways it never stops. It should become a congregational habit or lifestyle to think like this. Keep asking questions and sharing the answers with one another at Old First sessions. Soon, you'll feel the excitement mounting. Some may wish to jump right into a program; indeed you may be powerless to stop some changes. But we sincerely believe there is a second logical stage.

THE DESIGNING PHASE

Don't underestimate the necessity of taking time to change the climate. Begin to sort through the many things that could be done, and start prioritizing the things that should be done. Dare we say it: "Hurry slowly." Remember, a very important word of pastoral care: All change is experienced as loss. We did not say that all change is loss. We said that all change (even good, expected, positive change) is *experienced* as loss. That distinction is important.

We encourage pastors to join this process and become facilitators. Your visions are important, but not the only valid ones. Be the encourager, interpreter and communicator of what you are all learning as you go to school together in this process. Like muscle, decision-making can be a fragile process. In old churches, some old timers have had information control for a long time. A democratic process that activates the whole body of Christ, will seem like an unwarranted intrusion into their area of expertise. Develop pilot projects that have a beginning, and in due time, a review and evaluation process. When you learn what fits your theological tradition and emerging consensus, then begin to incorporate the results into your ongoing structure and program.

Many of us watched General Motors try rather unsuccessfully to change their whole huge company in order to compete with Japanese and European automobile production. They had limited success. Then, they freed up some people and money and created a whole new division called Saturn to develop a new car and a new production process. It was so successful that it created a cult following of sorts nationally among buyers and a remarkable *esprit de corps* among their formerly skeptical workers. Once Saturn had demonstrated that they could do it, then their learnings were able to be incorporated into the larger parent company with much less resistance. There's a parable here for old, tradition-bound structures. "You can do it!"

In the church we will work for permission to add, experiment, or change worship and communication patterns. We'll explore new ministry partnerships with artists or other affinity groups we find in city center. Obviously, if our own theological identity is fuzzy, we will be threatened by any partnerships. The insecurities of many old churches are pretty obvious. But it should also be clear that there are unique factors and boundaries around doctrine and practice that are good and should be reaffirmed. After careful inventories, it will be necessary to say "no" to some partnerships and ministry opportunities that are really very good things. But if the church is stretched too thinly and nothing is secure, it's easy to "burnout" our members.

Remember, it is the thesis of this book that there are some new advantages for old churches in this day when society is changing so quickly and no one seems to be in control of their own destiny. In this day of styrofoam cups and plastic culture, many young adults are flocking to ancient Anglican, Orthodox and Catholic churches, because at profound levels they promise *not* to change. Far from being a problem, tradition may be your salvation. Don't abandon it;

improve it. Remember this aphorism: Tradition is the living faith of the dead; traditionalism is the dead faith of the living. There is a difference. Will you discern it?

THE DOING PHASE

It has probably occurred to you that there are overlapping areas in all three phases we have described. Given the size and complexity of our churches, we will adjust accordingly. Moreover, we may find, as some churches have, that we will need to repeat this process every decade or so, given the drastic changes in our membership and the shifting generational values in our culture.

Many new groups have emerged in recent years with the specific agenda to help churches go through change processes. The Barna Group on the West Coast provides much helpful research and publications. The Leadership Network, originating in Tyler, Texas, has amazing resources and conferences focusing on creating and building vital congregations. Add to this the conferences and consultations of groups we all know about, and we are most blessed. There is no way our seminaries could prepare us for all these changes. Now life-long learning is both possible and necessary. Most Doctor of Ministry programs have sought to distill the best of these contemporary resources and integrate them into a theological and theoretical learning matrix for pastors. We should avail ourselves of all forms of peer and distance learning, while avoiding superficial cultural analysis. Some of us encourage the turning of cities like New York into major learning laboratories. It will soon be possible to link city center churches all over the world and learn from each other by the Internet.

Pastors Need Special Support Systems

Church Resource Ministries (CRM), is one of the contemporary organizations that has come along to help pastors by organizing them into small peer groups. They have done essentially what this book suggests should be done with congregations as a whole. These peer groups are multiplying quickly and have helped many pastors to clarify their own calling, vision and boundaries in ministry. Incidentally, CRM has also published their "short list" of characteristics of healthy congregations under the rubric of "natural church development."[1] CRM's eight characteristics include:

- visionary leadership
- gift mobilization
- passionate spirituality
- functional structures
- celebrative worship
- disciplemaking groups
- relational evangelism
- caring relationships

These are eight terrific qualities, but now that you've read this text, you will be tempted to add two more characteristics for renewing city center churches. They would be:

- a theologically-shaped identity, and
- a creative sense of contextualization in ministry

Both of these latter characteristics are unique contributions of this little book.

In sum, we will challenge old or traditional city center churches to proclaim the biblical idea that:

- God is interested in all of society; all communities and all social issues.

- God is at work in all history and is now active in the reconfiguring of city centers so that they can receive and link up the nations for active mission purposes in the third millennium.

- God is challenging the leadership of city center churches to take their personal faith into every public sphere linked to or located in the downtown marketplace, including the arts, medicine, politics, research, media, conventions, transit, courts, business and into the issues of every ethnic and cultural group.

- God requires pastors to equip lay members to articulate the gospel and deliver pastoral care to the hurting; and to reconcile the lost to God and to each other.

At their best, city center churches will recover the vision and dream like Isaiah (65:17f), for a more just and livable city and, while working with the powerful, never intentionally contribute to the ongoing marginalization of the powerless.

Yes, Old First churches did link too closely with the wealthy and powerful in their past. Too often they affirmed only one Eurocentric culture that required people to step through stained-glass to access Jesus. But, now that we have an urbanized world on all six continents, these old first churches at city center may find their new missiological role—as the global church which is also the local church. To such a vision, we commit them as we once again release this book.

The Future

In his *Four Quartets,* T. S. Eliot mused on the relationship between the past, present, and future:

> Time present and time past
> Are both perhaps present in time future,
> And time future contained in time past.*

Is there realistic hope for Old Firsts? We refer to Eliot's words because any consideration of the viability of the future must keep in mind the demands the past places on the present situation. There is an integral relationship between the viability of the future of Old Firsts and the seeds of their past. However, to be precise about the metaphor, we view the viability of the future not so much as determined by the seeds of the past, but by how the plants from those seeds are nurtured by present caretakers.

*From "Burnt Norton" in *Four Quartets* by T. S. Eliot, copyrighted by T. S. Eliot; renewed 1971 by Esme Valerie Eliot. Reprinted by permission by Harcourt Brace Jovanovich, Inc.

At any rate, to the question, "Is there hope for Old Firsts?" one could answer in one of two ways: "No, because…" or "Yes, if…." The latter formulation is the option we affirm.

We believe the conditions for renewal depend upon specific factors:

1. The character and quality of the leadership, both lay and clergy.

2. The determination and ability of the congregation to re-energizing itself, using sound biblical theology, values, goals and program commitments.

3. The extent to which the historical uniqueness and identity of churches can become conscious and functional guidelines for contemporary action.

4. The ability to uncover the dynamics and changing nature of their unique context and their willingness to confront it with realism, hope, and congruent models of caring.

5. The willingness of the congregation to make an inventory of God's gifts to them as God's people and the willingness to be fired up for their visions and ministries even if they do not fit the mold of previous programs.

6. The ability to develop and prioritize creative programming that is consistent with mission and not merely maintenance oriented.

7. The ability to change the organizational structure or forms in ways that enable new ministries to emerge and grow.

8. The ability to develop a process for bringing about change in the church, and the development of a caring network of church support systems that provide resources and assistance to help congregations caught in their environmental traumas.

The first seven conditions have been discussed in previous chapters of this book. The last condition was touched upon briefly in the last chapter when we issued a challenge to denominational leadership to deploy resources for facilitating renewal of Old Firsts. A bit more reflection on the impact these conditions might have on the future may be useful.

In our chapter on the history of Old Firsts, we suggested the *intentional* and *purposive* posture of the founders of these churches. It was as if they felt the eyes of destiny gazing intently on their backs as they labored relentlessly to plant a church in sometimes less than ideal circumstances. T. S. Eliot is right: time future is contained in time past to the extent that persons in the past are mobilized by the pull of the future and by the tug of destiny. First, nothing will change unless the people of Old Firsts have the will to live out their purpose under God and make the above conditions happen! Second, these conditions are not likely to be fulfilled if the friends of Old Firsts do not care enough to lend hands of support. Among these friends are community organizations made to feel comfortable in using the church's facilities, voluntary associations sharing the agony of working to feed the hungry and care for the outcasts, and community leaders sharing the desire to keep civic improvement as a constant goal. All are allies in the struggle for decency and the betterment of communities.

Finally, although we feel in the present age the ebb and flow of flux and the constancy of change, there is an important aspect of tradition in the church that acts simultaneously as a means of encouraging Christians to live effectively in the present while retaining a link with the past. That element is apostolic succession. In a sense every member of an Old First church lives out this doctrine. Members of Old Firsts receive the mantle of faith from unseen spiritual ancestors and prepare to pass it on to generations who will likewise never be seen with physical eyes. Thus every Old First powerfully embodies the rich heritage of the past, the mandate to live faithfully in the present, and the hope of being called "blessed" by future generations. May it ever be so.

Notes

Preface

[1]Joel Garreau, *Edge City* (New York: Doubleday, 1991).

Chapter 1

[1]Edwin Scott Gaustad, *A Religious History of America* (New York: Harper and Row Publishers Inc., 1966), p. 65.

[2]*Ibid.*

[3]Case history of First Baptist Church, Boston, Massachusetts.

[4]Case history of First Baptist Church, Philadelphia, Pennsylvania.

[5]Case history of Hamilton Square Baptist Church, Trenton, New Jersey.

[6]Case history of Flemington Baptist Church, Flemington, New Jersey.

[7]Case history of First Baptist Church, Hamilton, New York.

[8]Case history of First Baptist Church Ossining, New York.

[9]Case history of First Baptist Church: Oneonta, New York.

[10]Case history of First Baptist Church, Watertown, New York.

[11]Case history of First Baptist Church, Hamilton, New York.

[12]Case history of First Baptist Church, Mount Vernon, New York.

[13]H. Shelton Smith, Robert T. Handy, and Lefferts A. Loetscher, eds., *American Christianity, 1820-1960,* vol. II (New York: Charles Scribner's Sons, 1963), p. 10.

[14]Case history of First Baptist Church, Mount Vernon, Ohio.

[15]Case history of First Baptist Church, Parkersburg, West Virginia.

[16]Case history of Abyssinian Baptist Church of Harlem, New York City, New York.

[17]Case history of Second Baptist Church, Columbus, Ohio.

[18]Case history of Shiloh Baptist Church, Sacramento, California.

[19]Case history of First Baptist Church, Boulder, Colorado.

[20]Case history of First Baptist Church, Minneapolis, Minnesota.

[21]Case history of First Baptist Church, Wichita, Kansas.

[22]Case history of First Baptist Church, Poughkeepsie, New York.

[23]Case history of Central Baptist Church, Boston, Massachusetts.

Chapter 2

[1]Case history of Hamilton Square Baptist Church, Trenton, New Jersey.

[2]Anonymous, "Town and Country Abroad and at Home," *The Nation* (May 15, 1966), p. 618.

Chapter 3

[1]Robert Gordis, *Koheleth: The Man and His World: A Study of Ecclesiastes* (New York: Schocken Books, 1968).

[2]Case history of Bethel Baptist Church, Bethel, Ohio.

[3]Case history of First Baptist Church, Geneva, New York.

[4]Case history of First Baptist Church, Hamilton, New York.

[5]Case history of Pine City Baptist Church, Pine City, New York.

[6]Case history of First Baptist Church, Schenectady, New York.

Chapter 4

[1]Case history of First Baptist Church of Philadelphia, Pennsylvania.

[2]Case history of Abyssinian Baptist Church of Harlem, New York City, New York.

[3]Case history of First Baptist Church of Boston, Massachusetts.

[4]Case history of Second Baptist Church of Columbus, Ohio.

[5]Case history of First Baptist Church of Wichita, Kansas.

[6]Case history of First Baptist Church of Paterson, New Jersey.

[7]Case history of First Baptist Church of Poughkeepsie, New York.

[8]Case history of First Baptist Church of Parkersburg, West Virginia.

[9]Case history of Bethel Baptist Church of Bethel, Ohio.

[10]Case history of First Baptist Church of Mount Vernon, Ohio.

[11]Case history of First Baptist Church of Watertown, New York.

[12]Case history of Whitesboro Baptist Church of Whitesboro, New York.

[13]*Ibid.*

[14]Case history of Calvary Baptist Church of Washington, DC.

[15]Amitai Etzioni, *Modern Organization* (Englewood Cliffs, NJ.: Prentice-Hall, 1964).

Chapter 5

[1]The places to read about the social consequences of the Reformation are legion, but three starter sources could include the classic by Max Weber, *The Protestant Ethic and the Spirit of Capitalism* (New York: Charles Scribner's Sons, 1954); Karl Holl, *The Cultural Significance of the Reformation* (Cleveland: World Publishing, Co., 1959); or Georgia Harkness' fine study, *John Calvin: the Man and his Ethics* (Nashville: Abingdon Press, 1958), especially chapters 8 through 10 where, among many practical issues, she deals with Calvin's "secular vocation as divine calling."

[2]In a fascinating study, *The Culture of Professionalism: The Middle Class and the Development of Higher Education in America* (New York: W. W. Norton and Company, Inc., 1976), Burton J. Bledstein discusses the background factors that promoted a shift from Jacksonian democracy to Victorian professionalism democracy in the nineteenth century. While the book deals with colleges and seminaries directly, by implication it helps us understand why Old Firsts emerged as cultural bastions of America, for better or for worse.

[3]Abyssinian Baptist Church, "Keeping Faith: A Brief History of the Abyssinian Baptist Church."

[4]From case history of Second Baptist Church of Columbus, Ohio. An interesting aspect of this congregation is the fact that the membership profile shows that only 6 percent are over 50 years of age; 52 percent are between 25 and 45 years of age. The church is a leading influence in the city of Columbus.

[5]From case history of First Baptist Church of Minneapolis, Minnesota.

[6]From case history of First Baptist Church of Wichita, Kansas.

[7]From case history of First Baptist Church of Paterson, New.lersey.

[8]From case history of First Baptist Church of Lowville, New York.

[9]From case history of First Baptist Church of Elmira, New York.

Chapter 6

[1]Suggested by Stott in a lecture on leadership delivered at the Seminary Consortium for Urban Pastoral Education (SCUPE), Spring, 1983.

[2]Case history of the First Baptist Church of Washington, Pennsylvania.

[3]Case history of the First Baptist Church of Plainfield, New Jersey.

[4]Robert K. Greenleaf, *Servant Leadership: A Journey into the Nature of Legitimate Power and Greatness* (Ramsey, NJ: Paulist Press, 1977).

Chapter 7

[1]These models are based on those which have been used by Raymond Bakke in a variety of seminary and church consultations in recent years. See also the classic formulation of typology of religious collectivities in Ernst Troeltsch, *The Social Teachings of the Christian Churches* (Chicago: University of Chicago Press, 1981).

[2]This vignette about Ford is cited in Amitai Etzioni's helpful book, *Modern Organization* (Englewood Cliffs, NJ: Prentice-Hall, Inc., 1964).

Epilogue

[1]Church Resource Ministries, *Focusing Leaders* (Anaheim, CA: Church Resource Ministries), p. 5.